Lifegiving

Lifegiving
A Discovery Journal for
a Beautiful Life

TAMMY MALTBY
WITH TAMRA FARAH

MOODY PUBLISHERS
CHICAGO

Some material in this book is taken from *Lifegiving,* copyright © 2002 by Tammy Maltby, published by Moody Publishers.

All Scripture quotations, unless otherwise indicated, are taken from the *Holy Bible, New International Version®*. NIV®. Copyright © 1973, 1978, 1984 by International Bible Society. Used by permission of Zondervan Publishing House. All rights reserved.

Scripture quotations marked NASB are taken from the *New American Standard Bible®*, Copyright © The Lockman Foundation 1960, 1962, 1963, 1968, 1971, 1972, 1973, 1975, 1977, 1995. Used by permission.

Scripture quotations marked KJV are taken from the King James Version.

Scripture quotations marked NLT are taken from the *Holy Bible, New Living Translation,* copyright © 1996. Used by permission of Tyndale House Publishers, Inc. Wheaton, Illinois 60189. All rights reserved.

Produced with the assistance of The Livingstone Corporation (www.LivingstoneCorp.com). Project staff includes Paige Drygas, Neil Wilson, Kirk Luttrell, Ashley Taylor, Mary Horner Collins, Rosalie Krusemark, and Greg Longbons.

Interior design by Mark Wainwright

Library of Congress Cataloging-in-Publication Data

Maltby, Tammy.
   Lifegiving : a discovery journal for a beautiful life / Tammy Maltby
with Tamra Farah.
     p. cm.
Includes bibliographical references and index.
   ISBN 0-8024-1361-7
   1. Christian women—Religious life. I. Farah, Tamra. II. Title
BV4527.M238 2004
248.8'43—dc22

                                    2003024597

1 3 5 7 9 10 8 6 4 2

Printed in the United States of America

TAMMY

I would like to dedicate this study to a delightful, lifegiving woman who loves God's Word deeply—my mother-in law, *Joyce Multby*. Thank you for loving and praying for your son.

To my dear friend *Erin O'Keefe*. You have taught me to press into the life that really is life. I enjoy laughing with you, girl, and I so love *Miss Katie,* my Korean Princess. Thank you for letting me be a part of her life.

And to my three sisters, *Trudy, Twyla, and Terri.* I am deeply blessed to follow in your steps. Sisters are just about the best thing around.

TAMRA

I dedicate this study to my precious family, where all my lifegiving begins, and to the Lord Jesus Christ, who is the source of all my lifegiving.

CONTENTS

ACKNOWLEDGMENTS

I would like to thank so many woman who have encouraged me in the creation of this study—and many of them are you, my dear readers! As I have had the privilege of speaking these truths across our nation, many of you have asked for a tool to spur you and your friends on toward love and good deeds (Hebrews 10:24). Well, here it is. Thank you for asking for it!

Thank you to my friend Tamra Farah, who added so much depth to this study. You are an excellent writer, Tamra. Thank you for taking another journey with me.

And of course, thanks to my dear husband, Butch, and our children, Mackenzie, Tatiana, Samuel, and Mikia. I am so in love with all of you! How I ever got to be your wife and the mother of such remarkable children is the most amazing mystery of all.

And with all my heart and passion:

Oh, my precious and beautiful Jesus, You are so gracious to me! It's You that I love, awesome Savior who restores this weary soul. My Lily of the valley . . . my bright and morning Star . . . oh Father, bring Your healing splendor and reveal Yourself again.

"Look not mournfully into the past. It comes not back again. Wisely improve the present. It is thine. Go forth to meet the shadowy future, without fear."

HENRY WADSWORTH LONGFELLOW, 19TH CENTURY AMERICAN POET

INTRODUCTION
TENDING THE GARDEN OF OUR HEARTS

I am so grateful that you have chosen to walk this amazing journey with me! I trust that you are pouring yourself a cup of steaming hot coffee (filled with ice cream and chocolate, of course) and that you have God's lifegiving Word in hand.

My heartfelt desire is that this study will be a place of freedom for you, of intrigue and adventure. After all, lifegiving is the most amazing and satisfying dance you can dance. It is liberty from a self-imposed life. Girl, it is freedom to really get up and do the tango!

This discovery journal was designed to follow along with the book *Lifegiving*. You can read the chapters in the book as you work through the corresponding weeks in the journal, but you don't have to have the book in order to use the journal.

Each week this journal will provide you with the opportunity to tend the garden of your life. You can use this study journal as a part of your personal Bible study, or each week's lesson can be completed before meeting together in a small group setting. There is "spade-work" for each one to do before meeting together in your small group for discussion. On the days leading up to your group study, go through the Scriptures and take time to thoughtfully answer the questions. Dig deep so the truths of Scripture can take root in your heart.

All of us who have participated in weekly Bible studies know that daily life can choke out the time needed to prepare. Laundry Mountain waits to be scaled, dirty dishes never end, errands demand our attention, and family members need us. Life happens, and often it requires diligence to carve out enough time to truly prepare our hearts.

As you till the soil of your heart and allow the seeds of Scripture to be deeply implanted, remember that you are not alone in the garden of your life. It is the Master Gardener Himself who is working in you and who will work through you. You are in His loving care. Don't be discouraged if you find stony ground in your heart or weeds in your soul—these are the cares of life, the hurts, the disappointments, the personal sins that keep the Word from having its way in us. But be faithful to take your spade and plow up the hard earth of your heart when necessary. Work together with the Gardener so that the good seed goes into the good ground of a soft and teachable heart. Take courage, dear friend. This is a study full of hope and life! You will see a harvest. Count on it.

As you will see, each lesson in this study is divided into three parts—Good Seed, Good Ground, and Good Fruit. The themes in each lesson develop more fully from one section to the next, helping you to go deeper in your study with each question.

GOOD SEED

In this first section, we will take time to look carefully into the Scriptures. The Word of God is like seed that we plant in our hearts. We must take time to interact with that Word, to think about it, to ponder what the Spirit is saying to us.

Recently I was preparing to work through a difficult time with a friend. There was a wedge in our relationship, like a boulder blocking our way down the garden path. I knew my own thoughts and actions were hurting our friendship. I went to the Word and found a list of verses related to our circumstances. I wanted to yield to the truths and allow them to shape my feelings, thoughts, and attitudes. I experienced the wonder-working power and healing of God's Word as my friend and I moved past that difficult time and into a sweet time together. In the strength of the Lord, the boulder was removed from the path, and now it has become a beautiful rock formation off to the side of the garden. What once blocked our way is now a testimony to the healing power of God's Word.

Dear friend, begin the sacred process of studying God's Word. Take His hand. He has much to show you—and the Word is the lamp that lights your way (Psalm 119:105).

GOOD GROUND

During your personal study time, you are walking with Christ through the garden of your life. At times your heart will be ready to receive the Word. It seems the soil is tilled and rich.

At other times the Gardener will reveal stony ground. It seems as if the seed of the Word falls on unreceptive soil. Don't be discouraged! Though this is difficult and there is work to do, yield to the Master Gardener. Allow Him to break up the fallow ground. Will it hurt? Yes, sometimes it will. But it is a sweet pain that leads to life. Yielding to the discipline of the spade is the first step toward an abundant harvest.

So think deeply while you are in the Good Ground section. As sin comes to mind—unforgiveness, resentment, bitterness, ungodly anger, or any other thing that may leave your heart hardened—confess it to your loving Savior and receive His forgiveness. It is that humility that prepares us for what He wants to teach us.

Good Fruit

In this third section, we will take some time to apply the truths we have studied in the lesson to our lives. Galatians 6:9 promises that we will reap a harvest of blessing if we don't grow weary and give up. There have been many times in my life and in my relationships when I have expected an immediate harvest. I often wonder, *Why aren't things better yet? Why in the world won't that person change (*smile*)?* The truth is, I have to wait. God is at work. Sometimes I just don't see it.

This lesson became very real to me this summer when my son Sam was at a boys camp in upstate New York. He had been gone for almost three weeks. Finally the day came for him to fly home. I had missed him so much and couldn't wait to throw my arms around him. (He is thirteen now, so I try to be a bit cooler about giving him a big kiss in public.)

Around noon I received a call from the camp saying Sam had missed his first flight. A few hours went by, and then the airline called to say that his next flight had been canceled, and he'd be on an even later flight. And can you believe it, *that* flight had a mechanical problem, and he was put on yet another flight! By this point I was going crazy. My sweet boy in New York for ten hours, just waiting for a way to get home. I called the airlines, checked on-line, tried to use our frequent flier miles—anything to get my boy home!

Around 5:00 P.M. Sam called. I was so happy to hear his voice. He said, "Mom, do you know I have been sitting here in New York for ten hours? Haven't you been worried about me? Don't you care that I'm not home?"

I thought I would die. "Of course!" I said. "Sam, I have been doing everything I can to get you home. I have been calling, e-mailing, fretting, telling your dad he should be fretting, too. You have been on my heart and mind all day. We are trying to find a way for you to come home soon!"

Right at the moment, the Holy Spirit said to me, "Tammy, my dear child, I do that for you all the time. You are stuck in some lonely, painful place in your life, and you don't know that I am working out everything for your good. And child, trust me—I am very aware, and I will bring you home." Yes, God is at work . . . especially when we don't see it.

How easy it is to give up on God's good seed when we think it has been buried so deep we will never see any fruit. We stare at the ground, looking for the shoots to pierce the earth. Or worse, we dig it up to check if there is any growth. Waiting can be a difficult process, but it is well worth our patience.

Dear friend, hold on to the promise. Be encouraged. Live the life of love that God intended you to live. It is there for your taking, and the gift is very real! Hang on . . . and when you think you can't hang on another moment, trust God. Life is on the way.

Know that I journey with you. I have walked this path and have oftentimes seen sparse growth in my own life. Yet other times I have seen one amazing bounty. So girl, you go for it! Live a life of love, and find passion and purpose in giving your life away!

I'll be dancing the tango with you each step of the way!

Touching Hearts, Touching Lives

LIFEGIVERS ARE BEAUTIFUL

"It is the glow within that creates beauty." Bonnie Green

The other day I received an announcement from a dear, longtime friend in California whose daughter is graduating from high school. I haven't seen little Hillary for ten years, so you can imagine the awe I felt as I opened the lovely embossed invitation to attend her ceremony and a photo dropped out. Hillary has grown up to be a truly beautiful young woman, yet she still has a hint of the little eight-year-old child I once knew.

Hillary's fits all the American standards of a beautiful face. She must have many people tell her that she looks like a Barbie doll. She has a perfectly straight nose, huge dark eyes, full lips, and high cheekbones. She is gorgeous!

But this description is not the total tale of her beauty. . . .

Those classically beautiful features may have struck me first, but they were not her most lasting or memorable qualities. Even in a photograph, Hillary's lifegiving spirit seemed to pour out from her eyes and wash over her face, creating a countenance that brought tears to my eyes. The hidden person of Hillary's heart gave her outer beauty an enduring quality. This young woman may have the added dimension of outer beauty (ah, she's blessed!), *but it is the quality of her spirit that makes her truly lovely.*

Have you ever been with an unattractive person, yet the "glow within" left you with the fragrance of true beauty? Or, in contrast, can you remember encountering a woman with outward beauty, yet the deadness in her eyes shrouded her face? Her features may be a perfect "10," but they are lifeless, lackluster from an inner dullness.

This week's study is about how *all* lifegiving women are beautiful! You will be lifted up and encouraged as you see that beauty can characterize your life, no matter what you think about your physical features. Possibly you have had the painful experience of never feeling you were beautiful. My dear friend, if that is the case, you are in good company. The prophet Isaiah is the only one who gives us an idea of what the Lord Jesus looked like. As we will see, His visage was a bit less "Hollywood" than the average "Jesus poster" would lead us to believe.

GOOD SEED

Modern technology has laid the red carpet of beauty before us, and many more women are stepping out on it than ever before. We have cosmetic dentistry, plastic surgery, state-of-the-art highlights and hair color, acrylic nails, BOTOX®, and enough varieties of cosmetics to make our heads spin. For generations and in every culture, women have sought to improve their outward appearance so they could look and *feel* more beautiful. It is innate within us to improve our appearance, to beautify and to be beautified. Hey, most of us will take all the help we can get!

As long as one's bank account holds out, modern solutions are available to correct our perceived physical defects. Then what? We have to ask ourselves, ladies, is that all there is to this thing called beauty? Whether it is the perfect lipstick or the perfect facelift, will it be enough to make us truly beautiful? And if our physical bodies are a canvas and modern beautification techniques the medium, how should we paint? What kind of biblical plumb line do we drop to assess the value of these beauty potions? Let's look into Scripture and discover the source and the expression of true and lasting beauty.

1. First, let's assess how we feel about our appearance. What don't you like about your outward appearance?

_____

_____

_____

2. How do you deal with that disappointment?

_____

_____

_____

3. Now, let's start to get God's perspective. Read Psalm 139:1–18. Choose five phrases from this passage that speak to you about how God relates to your physical being. Next to each phrase, jot down why it comforts your heart.

❖

❖

❖

❖

❖

There you are, a woman—how wonderful! How unique you are, not "made in Japan" but made in your mother's womb. A factory needs plenty of light; God was so smart he could make you in the dark. That cowlick of yours, the length of your toes, your upper lip—he made all of you, and you are therefore very special and precious. [1]

ANNE ORTLUND

---

4. In Ezekiel 16 the Lord uses an analogy of outward adornment to express His loving care for Jerusalem and her people. He describes His process of beautification in great detail. Read Ezekiel 16:1–14. Jot down a list of some of the outward adornments and care that God lavishes on His people. (Hey, I wouldn't mind really having some of these!)

❖

❖

❖

❖

❖

❖

❖

❖

5. What did God bestow on Jerusalem that made her beauty *perfect* (see Ezekiel 16:14)?

_____

_____

_____

True, Ezekiel 16 is not the adornment of an actual woman; it is the figurative adornment of God's people. But it still clearly shows us the difference between inner and outer beauty—discernment we all need!

6. After God favored, adorned, and beautified Jerusalem, what happened (see Ezekiel 16:15–19)?

_____

_____

_____

7. How did she allow her beauty to lose all its splendor?

_____

_____

_____

8. What did God say He would do because of her sin (see Ezekiel 16:35–43)?

_____

_____

_____

Beauty loses its God-given splendor when it becomes an end in itself, the focus, or the ultimate goal.

True Beauty

Referring to Jesus, Isaiah 53:2 says, "He had no beauty or majesty to attract us to him, nothing in his appearance that we should desire him."

9. Isn't it fascinating that God would allow us to peer through this prophetic window to see what our Savior looked like? Since He was not physically attractive, what does this tell you about the *source* of Jesus' impact on others?

_____

_____

_____

10. What does that tell you about the *source* of your impact on others?

_____

_____

_____

First Peter 3:3–6 says:

> "Your adornment must not be merely external—braiding the hair, and wearing
> gold jewelry, or putting on dresses; but let it be the hidden person of the heart,
> with the imperishable quality of a gentle and quiet spirit, which is precious in
> the sight of God. For in this way in former times the holy women also, who
> hoped in God, used to adorn themselves, being submissive to their own hus-
> bands; just as Sarah obeyed Abraham, calling him lord, and you have become
> her children if you do what is right without being frightened by any fear" (NASB).

Peter's words must have struck a chord with his audience, as they do even in our day. Consider
the culture that Peter lived in when he wrote those powerful words under the direction of the
Holy Spirit.

It has been said that the Roman women of the day were addicted to ridiculous extravagance in
the adornment of the hair. Someone once satirized these customs by saying, "The attendants will
vote on the dressing of the hair as if a question of reputation or of life were at stake, so great is
the trouble she takes in quest of beauty; with so many tiers does she load, with so many continu-
ous stories does she build up high on her head. She is as tall as Andromache in front; behind she
is shorter. You would think her another person." The hair was dyed and secured with costly pins
and with nets of gold thread. False hair and blonde wigs were worn.[2]

It is obvious that the issue is excessive or obsessive attention to the outward person and little
or no attention to the inward person. Wow! The picture of true beauty is coming into focus. It is
not just the outward but the concealed and the private heart that matters. These verses from
1 Peter 3 give us this clarity. God wants us to give a lot of our attention to the hidden person of
our heart, to the whole inner self.

11. Describe the hidden person of the heart as you understand it from this passage.

_____

_____

_____

12. Peter tells us to adorn our hearts with the "unfading beauty of a gentle and quiet spirit" (1 Peter 3:4, NIV wording). (The word *spirit* here means "disposition" or "temper.") Is this a quality that can be found in every woman? Why or why not?

_____

_____

_____

Hunt around for a dictionary and look up these words. (You can use a Bible dictionary too, if you have access to one.)

Meek

Quiet

Mild

Gentle

Now don't be misled here. God has made each of us very different. We're not all meant to be molded into one boring pattern. I am far from a passive, spineless, wimpy woman. (Now admit it—you're glad I brought this to the light!) Yes, God has called me to be a leader. However, as God moves us into places of leadership and serving, our mind-set must be one of humility, grace, and patience. These inner qualities keep us serving, loving, and pressing in to people's needs and pain. It is the inner self that truly reflects the power of the resurrected life.

Now go back over the definitions and turn those into prayers, asking God to grow these qualities in that hidden part of you.

Have you ever noticed that true beauty fades when a woman believes that her outer appearance is the end-all? Awhile back we interviewed actress Jennifer O'Neal on *Aspiring Women,* the television show that I cohost. Interestingly enough, though she was one of the most physically beautiful women of her time, what she saw back then when she looked in the mirror was a woman she hated, a woman she was ashamed of, one who just never measured up. It seemed as if she had everything. She was bone-thin and physically a true knockout, yet she was using a measuring stick that would never stop demanding more. She didn't know how to tap into the hidden person of the heart, and because of it her life was full of great pain and disappointment. When all is said and done, the truly beautiful woman adorns herself with the lasting beauty found in the hidden person of the heart.

13. What do you observe in yourself or in others who seem to focus only on outward adornment?

_____

_____

_____

14. What do you observe in yourself or in others who seem to focus on the hidden, secret, concealed person of the heart?

_____

_____

_____

Beauty for Ashes

To bestow on them a crown of beauty
instead of ashes,
the oil of gladness
instead of mourning,
and a garment of praise
instead of a spirit of despair.
They will be called oaks of righteousness,
a planting of the Lord
for the display of his splendor.

ISAIAH 61:3

I heard Marilyn Hickey, a pastor's wife and world-renowned Bible teacher, speak at a retreat recently. She pointed out something very important from this Isaiah 61 passage: There is an exchange system at work here. To get gladness you have to give up your mourning. You want praise? You have to give up on giving up. You want beauty? You have to give up your ashes.

Ashes are the disappointments in life. The things we have done that have crashed and burned. The things others have done against us. The bitter things, hurts and disappointments, that we dwell on or talk about all the time. There is no beauty in that!

I love this quote by Anne Morrow Lindbergh: "What makes us hesitate and stumble? It is fear, I think, that makes us cling nostalgically to the last moment or clutch greedily toward the next. . . . But how to exorcise it? It can only be exorcised by its opposite, *love.*" We must exchange our ashes and our fear for God's love for us. Then, and only then, can we really be free.

15. What are the ashes in your life?

_____

_____

_____

GOOD GROUND

Look again at the list of ashes in your life. Write a prayer below, and express in detail how you are giving all of these ashes to God. Pray it out loud, asking God to give you beauty for those ashes in your life.

16. Take a few minutes to wait in silence. Meditate on the Lord Jesus' giving you beauty—revealed by the inner quality of a quieted, trusting spirit—for each of these ashes. Write out any insights the Holy Spirit may bring to your mind as you do this.

_____

_____

_____

_____

_____

_____

_____

_____

_____

_____

O wounded feet, O famished eyes,
Is there no healing for anyone?
No spell to make the wayworn wise?
No hint of the Divine?
But if indeed we too might bear
The dying of the Blessed One;
But if indeed we too might wear
The Life of God's dear Son,
Oh would we, could we, choose to miss
For loveliest bud of garden born,
One blow of reed, one stab from this
Our Saviour's crown of thorn.[3]

—AMY CARMICHAEL

17. In your own words, what is the source of inner beauty?

_____

_____

_____

Romans 13:14 says, "Rather, clothe yourselves with the Lord Jesus Christ, and do not think about how to gratify the desires of the sinful nature." Imagine clothing yourself in Christ. First take off the "clothing of the flesh." These fleshly garments might look like . . .

Self-promotion

Self-gain

Self-protection

Bitterness

18. Write out three or four fleshly interests, thoughts, and desires that compete for your attention and affection.

_____

_____

_____

19. Now write out a description—as detailed as you can—of what it means to clothe yourself in Christ.

_____

_____

_____

First Timothy 2:9–10 says, "I also want women to dress modestly, with decency and propriety, not with braided hair or gold or pearls or expensive clothes, but with good deeds, appropriate for women who profess to worship God." When we do good deeds, we are beautifully dressed. You might feel self-conscious writing this out, but take a look in your spiritual closet, and write out what good deeds you are "clothing" yourself with. I think that this is such a wonderful concept— God sees us beautifully dressed when we are serving, loving, and giving our lives away. Hey, it's a whole lot cheaper than a snappy new wardrobe!

GOOD FRUIT

Think with me for a minute about Mother Teresa. By worldly standards, she would be considered physically inferior to other women. Leathery skin covered her face, and her body was stooped from age and years of serving and caring for others. Yet her Christ-kissed countenance testified to a powerful inner light—and that light was Christ.

Her simple appearance didn't keep her from appearing before kings, queens, and presidents. And before them, she spoke the truth and boldly proclaimed her God. In her book *Loving Jesus,* Mother Teresa spoke of the "distressing disguise of Jesus in the poor."[4] She went on to say, "This is why the crippled and blind, the lepers, the unwanted, and the unloveds are our brothers and sisters. See the goodness of God! It was not enough for him to feed us, to make himself one of us. He had to satisfy his own hunger for us: So he makes himself the hungry one. He makes himself the naked one. He makes himself the homeless one. And he said, 'Whatever you did for the least of these my brethren, you did it to me. For I was hungry and you gave me to eat' (Matthew 25:40)."

20. Who are the hungry, the poor, the naked, and the oppressed in your life? (Believe it or not they are everywhere around you. Sometimes they are living in your own house.)

_____

_____

_____

21. Write out a prayer asking the Lord how you can serve Him by serving "the least of these."

_____

_____

_____

_____

_____

_____

_____

Did any ideas or people come to mind? Keep pondering this by praying this prayer. God will someday surprise you with an answer.

Living Beautifully

Perhaps you are wondering, Can I really be a woman like this? How do lifegivers find passion to give to others when their lives abound with big demands on their limited time? Can I really live a beautiful life?

22. What have you learned from the ideas in this week's lesson that will help you live beautifully this week?

_____

_____

_____

23. What steps can you take to cultivate the inner person of your heart this week?

_____

_____

_____

24. What are a few "good works" that you can clothe yourself in this week? List them, and experi-
    ence the joy and passion that comes from actually doing them!

_____

_____

_____

JOURNAL NOTES

JOURNAL NOTES

JOURNAL NOTES

_____
_____
_____
_____
_____
_____
_____
_____
_____
_____
_____
_____
_____
_____
_____
_____
_____
_____
_____
_____
_____
_____
_____
_____
_____
_____
_____
_____
_____
_____
_____
_____
_____
_____
_____

JOURNAL NOTES

Beauty by Design

Lifegiving Began in a Garden

Good Seed

Are you ready to discover why you have such a passion for beauty—why your heart stirs when you walk past an exquisite garden, why you linger over interior design magazines, and why getting a great pedicure can cure a month of ills?

Well, hold on, because what the Lord has shown me in this chapter might help you to understand a few of these longings and desires. It might unlock for you a few mysteries of why you are the way you are and Who intended you to be that way!

Let's read the key passage for this week's lesson together:

> The Lord God formed the man from the dust of the ground and breathed into his nostrils the breath of life, and the man became a living being. Now the Lord God had planted a garden in the east, in Eden; and there he put the man he had formed. . . . The Lord God said, "It is not good for the man to be alone. I will make a helper suitable for him.". . . So the Lord God caused the man to fall into a deep sleep; and while he was sleeping, he took one of the man's ribs and closed up the place with flesh. Then the Lord God made a woman from the rib he had taken out of the man, and he brought her to the man.
>
> Genesis 2:7–8, 18, 21–22

I know that many of you have read the Creation account a thousand times. You wonder, *What new things can I really discover that I didn't learn in Sunday school?* Watch!

1. From what did God form man?

_____

2. What did God plant in the east?

_____

3. Who did God put in the garden? (Notice that he was put there *after* he was created. Now did you really know that? I always thought he was created *in* the garden. And I was even on the Bible quiz team!)

_____

4. What did God conclude about man?

_____

_____

_____

5. What did God do to solve this?

_____

_____

_____

6. What did He do with the woman after He took her out of the man?

_____

_____

_____

7. Where was woman created?

_____

8. Do you see anything in these verses that might give us a clue about our natural inclination toward beauty, flowers, greenery, and fine and lovely things?

_____

_____

_____

I have concluded that *where* we were created has greatly impacted our identity as women. Of all the wonderful places God could have chosen to create a woman, He chose the center of the most beautiful place this earth has ever known! The botanical gardens didn't have a thing on the Garden of Eden.

Think of it—perfected beauty! The moment Eve opened her eyes she saw flawless beauty. When she tasted scrumptious fruits and smelled the loveliest lilies, when she touched the mane of a lion or heard the music of the sparrow, something connected. Something stuck. She loved this, and it gave her life. She was created *in* beauty and *for* beauty, and as women, our souls find their greatest passion and satisfaction when we are living lives of beauty and purpose.

9. Have you ever noticed that *most* men and *most* women beautify their surroundings differently? Think back to your college days! Ever been in a guy's dorm room? A bachelor pad and a woman's nest can feel very different inside. Think of a few examples that illustrate this difference.

_____

_____

_____

_____

Lifegiving began in the garden, but so did death. Read Genesis 2:16–17 and 3:1–5. Let's take a look at how the beauty of the Garden lost its luster. God commanded Adam (and Eve through Adam) not to eat of the Tree of the Knowledge of Good and Evil. Not long afterward, Adam and Eve disobeyed God, and death came into the Garden.

10. Adam and Eve did not physically die at that moment. How did death come into the world through their decision to disobey God (see Romans 5:12)?

_____

_____

The "Genesis 3 Choice" that humans made is called the Fall. Nothing has been quite as beautiful in this sin-scarred world since then. Sin affected us, our environment, our relationship with God, and even our relationships with each other. One of the most painful results for us as women is in the area of broken relationships and dashed hopes. In the story of Hannah in 1 Samuel 1:1–2:11, we see plenty of both. But we also see beauty restored when God answers Hannah's heart cry and gives her the desire of her heart. Take a few minutes to read this passage and meditate on it.

11. Describe the broken relationships Hannah experienced in this passage.

_____

_____

12. Why did Peninnah provoke Hannah?

_____

_____

13. What was Hannah's husband's response?

_____

_____

14. Using words from Scripture, describe how Hannah dealt with her distress (see 1:10–11, 15).

_____

_____

15. What did the priest think when he saw her?

_____

_____

16. How did the Lord answer Hannah's prayer?

_____

_____

17. What was Hannah's response?

_____

_____

18. Scripture records the songs of several women, and Hannah's is one of them. (Two others are Miriam's song and Mary's Magnificat.) List the most meaningful phrases to you from Hannah's song and explain why each is meaningful to you.

   ❖

   ❖

   ❖

   ❖

   ❖

Hannah experienced God's restoration. The before and after picture of her life makes a striking contrast. God transformed her from a broken, depressed, defeated woman into a happy, fulfilled, and thankful woman. In Isaiah 41:17–20 we see another picture of God's restoration. Read these verses and then respond to the questions below.

19. What are the poor and needy doing?

_____

20. How does God respond?

_____

21. What does He open on barren heights?

_____

22. What does He bring into the valleys?

_____

23. Into what does He turn the desert?

_____

24. Into what does He make the parched ground?

_____

25. What is God's purpose in doing all of this?

_____

_____

_____

Good Ground

Let's look back now on the passages we've studied this week and see what lessons we can draw from them.

26. The whole world changed when Adam and Eve sinned. Sin and death entered the world and affected the entire human race. How does the disobedience of Adam and Eve still affect us today . . .

in our relationships?

_____

in our activities?

_____

in the spheres in which we live (homes, workplaces, the environment, etc.)?

_____

27. When Hannah felt distressed, she turned first to the Lord. Be honest with yourself. What is the first thing *you* do when you experience relational distress or disappointment? Think of a specific example.

_____

_____

_____

28. Ask the Lord to help you develop a "Hannah Habit" when it comes to dealing with distress and disappointment. How could we define a Hannah Habit? List as many specific ideas and steps as you can. Refer back to 1 Samuel for phrases that described Hannah's response.

_____

_____

_____

   In the Isaiah 41 passage, we saw what God can do in barren places, valleys, deserts, and dry places. Many of us—because of our own sinful choices or the sins of others against us—experience these things in our souls. Though this may take a few minutes and be a bit painful, I encourage you to allow the Holy Spirit to reveal these places to you.

29. Describe the parched and barren places in your soul in as much detail as you can in the left column.

BARREN, DRY, PARCHED PLACES	RIVERS, SPRINGS, POOLS OF WATER

   Now go back through the list, and in the right column write out a prayer asking God to bring His river of provision to these hurting places of your life. If He has already done that, write down a testimony of how He did that in your life.

   Notice that all of God's provisions in this Isaiah passage come in the form of water! Water is essential to physical life; it refreshes and sustains us, and we cannot survive without it. Nothing else quenches our thirst quite like water. Water is also essential to spiritual life, and God uses the metaphor of living water to illustrate how He refreshes us spiritually.

30. Read John 4:7–14. Here Jesus encounters a woman at a well and tells her about the living water that He offers. What does it mean to receive His living water in your life? Describe how you have experienced this.

_____

_____

_____

GOOD FRUIT

Every day we are exposed to cultural messages that encourage us to suppress our lifegiving nature. We're told we should ignore our natural instincts to give and nurture life. The feminist movement that began a few decades ago gave voice to these new ideals. Radical feminist Gloria Steinem called the impulse in women to make sacrifices for others—to nurture and care for others—a "compassion disease." Other messages are less blatant but equally destructive. We're told that caring for others is less important than caring for ourselves, pursuing our own careers and selfish ambitions, embracing sexual "freedom" and a unisex brand of "equality." We've grown accustomed to hearing the world's brand of womanhood, but the truth is that God did not create us this way. Yes, women are equal to men; but we are not men! God designed us to be uniquely different.

We must fix our minds on Christ and renew our minds with His truth (Romans 12:2). This will enable us to discern the impact cultural messages have on our hearts and lifestyle. Those of us who grew up under the cloud of feminism may not readily identify some of these messages as lies. We must step into the light in order to see the truth. Compassion is not from disease; it is by design!

31. Describe how your thinking may have been impacted by these negative messages from society.

_____

_____

_____

32. We have been called to nurture life around us, to raise life above mere existence. List three things you did last week that sprang from compassion in your heart. Nothing is too small to list!

   ❖

   ❖

   ❖

33. What are three new ways you can cultivate beauty in your relationships?

   ❖

   ❖

   ❖

34. Write out a prayer to God, asking Him to help you put these principles into practice:
   • That you will pour out your deepest desires and disappointments to Him in prayer, as Hannah did.
   • That you will surrender your dry, barren places to Him so that you can receive His living water.
   • That you will discern and tune out incorrect cultural messages and live compassionately and beautifully in His sight.

_____

_____

_____

_____

_____

_____

JOURNAL NOTES

JOURNAL NOTES

JOURNAL NOTES

Small Offerings Lead to a Bountiful Harvest

The Power of the Seed

Have you ever opened your closet, been faced with a jumble of clothes, and closed the door quickly so that nothing would fall out on your head? When we discover a mess, it's natural to turn away and tell ourselves that we'll deal with it later. The piles are too high, the disorder too great, the chaos overwhelming. This is how we sometimes feel about the fallout of sin in our lives, too. We may have repented of the sin, but to face the tangled web that sin created in our souls, minds, and relationships may seem like too much to handle.

Zechariah 4:10 encourages us not to "despise these small beginnings" (NLT). Any thousand-mile trip begins with one step. Though we may not start out with mastery—whether it is in our thought life or in a skill like cooking—to head in the right direction we must *begin*. Start simply, but simply start.

This is true for every potentially lifegiving relationship, whether it be a difficult marriage, a strained friendship, a sour teacher at school, a cantankerous family member. Small offerings of love are seeds that we plant, and we will reap a harvest of blessing if we don't give up (Galatians 6:9).

Good Seed

One day a sinful woman came to Jesus. Many people *came to see* Jesus; only some really *came to* Him in true repentance. This woman didn't just mosey up to Jesus while He was walking along a road. She braved a very intimidating, shameful situation to get to Him. And when she got there, she was less than timid about how she approached Him. Get ready to really see Jesus, the strong Defender and Lover of our souls that He really is. I just love this story.

1. Read Luke 7:36–50. Whose house did the sinful woman enter?

_____

_____

_____

The Pharisees were the chief accusers of the day. These men were ruthless. Their goal was to make everyone (except themselves, of course) afraid of God and filled with shame. Listen to what Jesus said about them. I love that Jesus doesn't mince words—what a hero He is to me!

> "You hypocrites! Isaiah was right when he prophesied about you:
> 'These people honor me with their lips,
> but their hearts are far from me.
> They worship me in vain;
> their teachings are but rules taught by men.'"
>
> MATTHEW 15:7–9

What courage He displayed when He confronted them so boldly. And if you think that's all He said, check out these verses from Matthew 23 too. I think we can safely conclude that Jesus took serious issue with the lives and hearts of the Pharisees.

"Woe to you, teachers of the law and Pharisees, you hypocrites! You shut the kingdom of heaven in men's faces. You yourselves do not enter, nor will you let those enter who are trying to" (23:13).

"You blind fools!" (23:17).

"You blind men!" (23:19).

"Woe to you! . . . You give a tenth of your spices. . . . But you have neglected the more important matters of the law—justice, mercy and faithfulness" (23:23).

"Woe to you! . . . You are like whitewashed tombs, which look beautiful on the outside but on the inside are full of dead men's bones and everything unclean" (23:27).

"You snakes! You brood of vipers! How will you escape being condemned to hell?" (23:33).

I think He just threw that last one in for good measure!

Now, back in Luke 7, picture with me this prostitute entering the home of a Pharisee . . . yes, his _personal house, his domain, his space,_ in order to see the Giver of all life.

2. Knowing the hostile atmosphere of the house she was about to enter, what do you think motivated this woman to overcome her fears?

_____

_____

_____

If you answered that she was desperate, without hope, lost in the sin she had committed and in sin that was done against her, then I think you're on the right track. I think she was frantic, and this was her last-ditch effort at life.

3. What did she do when she got to Jesus?

_____

_____

_____

4. What did the Pharisee say about her?

_____

_____

_____

The Value of Compost

This brings us to a fascinating point, and it has been life-changing for so many women I teach. I once spoke at a women's conference about living a beautiful life. I was sharing with these women that the garden of our lives can be so beautiful that the world will be intoxicated by its fragrance and beauty, which, of course, is Christ Himself. Well, the women there had so much brokenness in their lives that they couldn't even begin to think of living beautifully. They were barely making it in survival mode. Have you ever been there—hardly able to get though the day? I know I have.

I went back to my room that night, and God showed me something very powerful. He told me to go back to my gardening books to see what creates really beautiful gardens. And do you know what it is? Compost! And what is compost? Waste. Dung. It is something dead that was once alive, and through being tilled into the soil, it has the potential to bring forth the most amazing beauty and life. It is the key ingredient. How amazing is it that compost actually has life-changing value!

Now get this. When the sinful woman entered the house to approach Jesus, the Pharisee said to himself, "If this man were a prophet, he would know who is touching him and what kind of woman she is—that she is a sinner" (Luke 7:39). In the original Greek, what the Pharisee was really saying was that if Jesus knew what kind of "dirt" this woman was, what kind of "dung" she had in her life, then He would have nothing to do with her.

Yet wild as it seems, it was her acknowledgment of her "compost" or sin that brought her life. Humble repentance was the most important heart ingredient. Jesus took the compost of her life and created a life of beauty—not *in spite of* it but *out of* it! The reason she loved much was because she had been forgiven much. Let that sink in.

That means that all of our brokenness can be used to bring forth true life in us. It means that nothing is wasted! It means that no matter the sin, shame, or secret, once it is given to Jesus, the ultimate Lifegiver, we'll receive beauty for our ashes, acceptance for our shame.

What an amazing friend we have in Jesus! Sister, this can be the beginning of true freedom over your past. Give Jesus all your compost. Offer it to Him. He is waiting. He will make something beautiful out of it.

5. List some areas of compost that you want to release today. I have found that most life compost is the result of rejection, shame, and unforgiveness—sins done against us and sins we have committed. Dig deep. Confess your sin, repent of it, and hand it over to God.

_____

_____

_____

Remember, don't rush through this. It can change your life. I have even known women who wrote down their compost, ripped it up, and buried it in their backyards. That's a symbolic act you'll never forget.

6. Let's return to the story. Read Luke 7:40–50. What was Jesus' response to the Pharisee?

_____

_____

_____

7. What does this story reveal about Jesus' attitude toward sinners who come to Him?

_____

_____

_____

8. How did Jesus receive this woman, and how did He measure her sin?

_____

_____

_____

9. List three ways she could have approached Jesus that would have been more "upstanding" or "dignified"?

_____

_____

_____

10. What does it tell you about Jesus that though she did not approach Him in that way, He still received her?

_____

_____

_____

New Life

Let's look together at what God can do through small beginnings. Read Isaiah 43:18–19.

11. How are we supposed to relate to "former things" (such as past sin in our own lives or ways others have sinned against us)?

_____

_____

_____

12. What kinds of "new things" does God begin in our lives?

_____

_____

_____

GOOD GROUND

What does the story of the sinful woman show us about how we can approach Jesus, even if we have lived lives of blatant, shameful sin? Our Luke 7 friend shows us that a broken and desperate heart condition is the key to beginning a life of love. Whether your sins seem small or great, you cannot approach Christ without humility.

As a host on the show *Aspiring Women*, I get to hear some amazing stories of how God can turn around any life surrendered to Him. We interviewed a woman recently who was a former stripper, prostitute, drug addict, and alcoholic—all by the age of twenty-one. Not only that, but she had also been gang-raped, hospitalized after several drug-overdose attempts, and was the mother of a young child. I guess you could say she was living—well, maybe more like barely *surviving*—in the cesspool of rejection, shame, and sin.

But one day, through the most amazing chain of events, she saw a church, and with tears streaming down her face, she ran inside. She cried out to God to have mercy on her, lit a candle, and put a one-hundred-dollar bill near it (which she had just turned a trick to get). Yet in the midst of her sin and shame, God heard her and brought a lifegiving woman into her desperate life. You wouldn't believe who this woman is today! She now works with the very same type of broken women that she used to be. When she told us her story, she sadly reported that all the other girls she had prostituted and stripped with were now dead. It's so amazing that there is simply no place God cannot reach to change a life!

A modern-day Luke 7 woman? I think so. She knew her need and reached out for mercy to the Giver of all life, Jesus Christ. Perhaps you find it hard to imagine living such a life of sin and brokenness. The truth is that is how God sees *all* our sin. Regardless of how "much" sin you have, your sin separates you from God. There are no exceptions to this rule. We are all sinners in need of a forgiving God.

Sometimes approaching God isn't nearly as difficult as moving past those who heap shame upon us. The Luke 7 woman had to press past her chief accusers to reach Jesus.

13. Do you ever feel you have to press past those who remember your sin, judge you for it, and just can't seem to let it go? Have you ever been rebuffed by a pharisaical type of Christian? Describe that experience (and trust me, I know it was painful).

_____

_____

_____

   I remember that when I went through my divorce at the age of twenty-three, one person very close to me at the time said, "God will never use your life. You are shelved and a disgrace of a Christian." It took me nearly twenty years to discover that was *not* God speaking but rather a modern-day Pharisee.

   Sometimes we have to intentionally meditate on who Christ really is and how He receives sinners, as shown in His Word, in order to see how different that is from the way some people, who say they are Christians, may treat us. Not everything done in Christ's name is from Christ, and some Pharisees today hide behind the Lord's name in order to justify how cruelly they treat others. Can you take a minute to forgive that person who rejected you? You may need to spend a few minutes meditating on how Jesus receives you when you turn from your sin to Him.

14. Describe how you would approach Jesus today—even though you may feel you have sinned against Him terribly. Keep the Luke 7 woman's example in mind. What would that look like for you?

_____

_____

_____

15. How do you think Jesus will receive you when you come to Him?

_____

_____

_____

   Remember, it is the smallest seed placed in the hand of the Master Gardener that, when planted, brings forth true life. Even your act of coming to Him as this young prostitute did is the first seed. He will plant your obedience. He is faithful.

16. In Mark 4:30–32, we read the story of a mustard seed that, when planted and tended, became a large tree, which in turn became a place for birds to nest and rest. How is this a picture of our lives in Christ?

_____

_____

_____

17. When we plant seeds of the Word of God in our lives and in the lives of others, what can those seeds grow up to become?

_____

_____

_____

Growth doesn't happen overnight. This process requires our patience. It may take days, weeks, months, even years before we see the fruit of the seeds we've planted. And the time of waiting may not always be easy.

18. According to Psalm 126:5, how do you feel when you are sowing? Describe a time in your life when you were planting seeds—in a circumstance or in a relationship—and it was so hard you cried your way through it.

_____

_____

_____

19. What was the outcome of those acts of lifegiving love over time? Did you "reap in joy," or are you still waiting? (Sometimes you have to wait a long time.)

_____

_____

_____

GOOD FRUIT

20. How have you planted small, lifegiving seeds in the lives of others? List three examples.

   ❖

   ❖

   ❖

21. What have you been thinking about doing lately that would be a small lifegiving act, but you have been putting it off? Why have you been putting it off? (If you are really struggling with getting started in sowing good seeds, ask a friend to pray for you.)

   _____

   _____

   _____

22. Describe a time when you saw God bless a small beginning.

   _____

   _____

   _____

23. Think back to an experience you've had in your relationship with the Lord where you experienced His love and forgiveness, as the sinful woman did in Luke 7 (even if you just experienced it this week). What was that experience like?

   _____

   _____

   _____

Let's end this week with a promise of hope. May it encourage you to sow small seeds and patiently wait to see God bring forth new life. From one compost-laced woman to another, let me remind you that "all things work together for the good of those who love God and have been called according to His purposes" (Romans 8:28). What hope we have! What a promise and a future! Bless you, dear friend.

He who began a good work in you will carry it on to completion until the day of Christ Jesus.

PHILIPPIANS 1:6

JOURNAL NOTES

JOURNAL NOTES

JOURNAL NOTES

JOURNAL NOTES

The Ultimate Lifegiver Is Tending Your Garden

The Good Gardener

There seem to be two extreme kinds of Christians—those who work too hard to be godly and those who don't work hard enough. The first kind tend to strive, always thinking they need to improve, often feeling condemned rather than convicted, having a hard time experiencing the love of the Father. Sadly, these people are often the victims of heavy circumstances—a broken home, an alcoholic parent, or some type of soul-searing abuse. Sometimes, though, this is just a person's natural tendency.

The other extreme type of Christian may have experienced some of the same traumas in life, yet she has responded very differently. This person bolsters herself with the view that she is usually right. She can't figure out why someone might have a problem with her. When she gets into a difficult situation, her first reaction is that the other person must be wrong—*she* certainly isn't! This type of person is usually slow to see sin in her own life and takes the laid-back approach to growth and change. Of course God loves her. Goodness me, why wouldn't He (smile)?

Neither extreme describes the dynamics of abiding in Christ. As we will see in this lesson, all fruitfulness begins with abiding—or remaining—in Him. Being a driven person, I'm often overly critical of myself and get caught up in overzealous self-improvement, so I was deeply struck the first time I saw the balancing truth in the following verses.

So then, my beloved, just as you have always obeyed, not as in my presence only, but now much more in my absence, work out your salvation with fear and trembling; for it is God who is at work in you, both to will and to work for His good pleasure.

PHILIPPIANS 2:12–13 (NASB)

On the one hand, I do have work to do! I have to work out the salvation God has given me. On the other hand, it is *God* who is working in me—and He's doing it for His pleasure! There is a message here for both extremes we described. If you tend to live as if your spiritual growth is all up to you, take heart. *He* is at work within you. If you tend to be a bit too laid-back, not thinking enough about what God may want you to do, realize that there's a fear and trembling, a deep reverence for God, that should snap you to attention. Your life is holy ground, a continual work in progress, a constant construction zone.

With these ideas as a backdrop, let's explore God's desire that we be more and more fruitful in His kingdom, which brings Him pleasure and gives us life.

GOOD SEED

In Luke 12:41–48 Jesus tells a parable about being faithful with what God has given us to do, regardless of our circumstances.

1. In this parable, what was the servant supposed to be doing?

_____

_____

_____

2. What will the master do for the servant who is faithful?

_____

_____

_____

3. In contrast, examine what the unfaithful servant was thinking. "The servant said to himself, 'My master is taking a long time in coming'" (Luke 12:45). What does the servant mean by this?

_____

_____

_____

4. Write verse 47 below. What is the connection in this verse between what the servant *knew* and what the servant *did*?

_____

_____

_____

5. Notice in verse 48 that there is a different level of accountability for others. What's the difference?

_____

_____

_____

6. Write out Jesus' words, found in the second part of verse 48, that sum up this parable.

_____

_____

_____

Abiding in Christ

Let's spend some time together on the concept of abiding. Turn now to John 15:1–9. This is a very significant passage about our life in and connection to Christ.

7. Based on these verses, we know that . . .

Christ is the _____.

The Father is the _____.

We are the _____.

8. In your own words, explain how these three images relate to each other.

_____

_____

_____

The Greek word for *abide* in this passage is *meno* (men´-o). It is a primary verb that means "*to stay* (in a given place, state, relation, or expectancy)." It means to continue, dwell, endure, be present, remain, stand, or tarry.[1]

9. What then does it mean to abide in Christ? How does this affect your relationship with Him?

_____

_____

_____

10. A significant principle in our Christian lives is *pruning*. Define what pruning is as a healthy gardening practice.

_____

_____

_____

11. Why does God the Father, the Gardener, prune the branches (you and me)?

_____

_____

_____

12. What is the ultimate result of remaining in Christ (see verse 8)? How is the Father glorified?

_____

_____

_____

This passage from John illustrates the importance of abiding in Christ. You are attached to Christ, the vine, who gives you life, and He dwells within you. This concept of abiding, or living within, is illustrated in an Old Testament passage as well.

"Enlarge the place of your tent,
stretch your tent curtains wide,
do not hold back;
lengthen your cords,
strengthen your stakes.
For you will spread out to the right and to the left;
your descendants will dispossess nations
and settle in their desolate cities."

ISAIAH 54:2–3

In this passage the effectiveness of our lives is described with the analogy of enlarging our tents. At one time the Israelites dwelled in tents. Expanding your tent meant that things were going well and that your prosperity (in family and in goods) was multiplying, so you needed more space to contain it.

13. The Israelites were encouraged to expect God's blessing and to figuratively enlarge the place of their tents. List the specific instructions God gave. Notice the verbs that Isaiah used in this passage and what they communicate.

Enlarge _____.

Stretch _____.

Do not _____.

Lengthen _____.

Strengthen _____.

14. What is God promising to the Israelites through these instructions?

_____

_____

_____

15. What is the underlying concept in this passage? Since we don't live in literal tents today, what does this passage communicate to us?

_____

_____

_____

16. How does the idea of enlarging your tent relate to the last concept we studied, abiding in the Vine?

_____

_____

_____

GOOD GROUND

Let's look back now on the passages we've studied and examine the lessons we can draw from them.

17. In Luke 12:45, we noticed that the unfaithful servant thought, "My master is taking a long time in coming," so he concluded that he didn't need to worry about his master's instructions. Describe a time when you felt convicted to obey God about something, but you said to yourself, "I'll get to that later. God won't mind!"

_____

_____

_____

18. John 15 showed us the relationship between the Vine, the branches, and the Gardener. Think now about the pruning process. How does God go about pruning us? Think of a few real-life examples of what we might experience when God is pruning us.

   ❖

   ❖

   ❖

That pruning process can feel terribly painful. For some, pruning might be losing a job, or rushing to the nursery because your perfect child just bit another child (yes, it happened!), or making a humbling mistake at work, or just outright failing in something you thought you could do.

I remember one of the most painful prunings in my life (and I have had many) was when I spoke at a big event, and I grabbed the wrong notes, dropped my Bible on stage, lost my place a time or two, and generally had a terrible time. I now believe God was trying to tell me, "Tammy, you are not abiding in Me. You, my dear child, are trying to survive and succeed in your own strength, and without Me you will fail! Apart from Me you can do nothing that really matters or lasts."

Oh, dear sister, did I learn that the hard way! But how grateful I am that I did. It has now freed me to embrace opportunities I would naturally be afraid of taking on. He continues to prune me so that as I decrease, He continues to increase (John 3:30).

19. Think back on some of your own life experiences. Describe a time when you were remaining in Christ, doing well, and bearing fruit, when all of a sudden it seemed like you were being "cut back."

_____

_____

_____

20. Be honest: Who did you blame? (Did it occur to you to blame the devil?) Looking back now, how do you see that experience?

_____

_____

_____

21. Return to the second illustration of abiding, enlarging your tent, that we read about in Isaiah 54. How would you like God to "enlarge the place of your tent"?

_____

_____

_____

22. What would you liken the stretching of the tent curtains to in your life? To what would you liken the lengthening of your cords? The strengthening of your stakes?

_____

_____

_____

Take special note of this: *To go out broader in influence, we must first drive our stakes down deeper.* I have had so many women say to me that they want to have a greater ministry and influence for the Lord. And I always respond, "Are you ready for the painful, long-term testing of it? Because as God promotes you to greater levels, your stakes will be tested at every turn." Everything that can be pulled up will be. Trust me. And how our stakes loosen their hold will look different to each of us.

My stakes get wobbly and loose when I don't spend enough time with the Lord, when I over-commit myself and feel stressed out. My tent stakes lose their power to hold my life in place when I have not made my husband, children, and our home a priority against the backdrop of opportunities (even good ones) and demands. I wish I could tell you the battles are few and far between, but they aren't—at least not for me. I must daily commit to nailing my stakes down securely. This requires a moment-by-moment awareness that I must protect what keeps me strong. But the good news is that as I do this, the winds of adversity and testing cannot pull those stakes out, no matter what comes my way. I can feel shaken (and often do), but I will not be undone.

23. So, dear friend, what does strengthening your stakes look like in your life? How can you guard this with all diligence?

_____

_____

_____

24. Have you spent too much time on other things—even good things—and not enough time on the home front?

_____

_____

_____

There's no shame here. We all need to take a hard look inward to make sure our lives are staked down securely. If you are feeling a bit undone, ask a good, faithful friend to help you evaluate your schedule and commitments. What you give your time and energy to says a lot about you. Sometimes a friend's faithful pruning can help you see the forest through the trees. Take a moment right now to ask God to help you discover what stakes need to go a bit deeper, what extra commitments need to go, and how to live free in the midst of life's busyness. He who began a good work in you will be faithful to complete it (Philippians 1:6). I cannot tell you how often I cling to that verse.

Be honest with God and yourself, repent where needed, and get to work nailing those tent stakes down a bit stronger. You'll be so glad you did!

GOOD FRUIT

Take a few minutes now to reflect on your life in Christ and your experience of abiding in Him.

25. Describe a time when you truly experienced what it was like to continue, dwell, and remain in Him. Was it during a happy or painful time?

_____

_____

_____

26. List some of the fruit that has resulted from your abiding in Christ. Don't feel shy. This is a private journal between you and God. Use this as an opportunity to glorify God for what He has produced in and through you.

_____

_____

_____

27. Describe the most poignant pruning experience you've ever had.

_____

_____

_____

28. Did you experience greater fruitfulness after a pruning experience? Why or why not?

_____

_____

_____

29. How does it affect your view of God to know that He is the Gardener and can and will prune you? Do you see Him differently because of that?

_____

_____

_____

   Let's close our time together by reflecting on these encouraging verses. He is the faithful and good Gardener!

Now the Lord is the Spirit, and where the Spirit of the Lord is, there is freedom. And we, who with unveiled faces all reflect the Lord's glory, are being _transformed into his likeness_ with ever-increasing glory, which comes from the Lord, who is the Spirit.

2 CORINTHIANS 3:17–18 (EMPHASIS MINE)

Therefore we do not lose heart. Though outwardly we are wasting away, yet inwardly we are being renewed day by day. For our light and momentary troubles are achieving for us an eternal glory that far outweighs them all.

2 CORINTHIANS 4:16–17

   Okay, sister, go for it! Let Him do His good work in your life—pruning and all—and watch the beauty that emerges from that. I only wish I could be there to see it!

JOURNAL NOTES

JOURNAL NOTES

JOURNAL NOTES

Journal Notes

Secret Giving Brings Eternal Rewards

THE SECRET PLACE

God's Word is amazingly clear: *He wants us to live our lives in front of Him and behind others' backs.* **He is an unseen God who sees our unseen actions. He is the One who rewards all acts done in secret, and He rewards them openly.**

Matthew 6:1–2 says that if we do our good works before people *to be seen by them* (rather than *to be seen by God*), then we have received our reward. Jesus is not telling us that it's wrong to be seen doing good to others; rather, He is saying that if our motivation is for the praise of others or for a reward from others, then that will be our full reward—their praise.

In contrast, if our intention is to be seen only by God, then our acts of service are beautiful to Him, and He will reward what the world cannot see.

After telling my husband about something I had done for someone else, he responded, "Isn't that great!" I thought about it and then said back to him, "Well, I have my reward." When I *seek* the praise of people and get it, then that is all I will get, so I'd better enjoy it. When I tell someone else about something that I did in secret that was meant to be "for God's eyes only," then my only reward is their accolade. I have given up my heavenly and eternal reward. With this passage, Jesus gives us a striking perspective change once again.

Secret service is not the only secret subject in Matthew 6. There is also secret prayer, secret forgiveness, and secret fasting. Again, as we pray and forgive others before our unseen God, He rewards us openly. As we fast before God alone (and we shall see that fasting is a very big idea to God), He is greatly moved on our behalf, and He will reward us—openly! (Hey, God said it, not me!)

GOOD SEED

1. Read Matthew 6:1–4. In your own words, summarize what Jesus was warning us to beware of.

_____

_____

_____

2. Are we to beware of anyone else ever seeing the good things we do, or are we just to beware of those things that we do to be noticed by others? What does this tell you about the importance of our motives?

_____

_____

_____

3. What do we lose when we do acts of righteousness to be seen by others?

_____

_____

_____

4. When we receive the honor of people, what have we also received in full?

_____

_____

_____

5. What does it mean to not let your left hand know what your right hand is doing? How is that possible?

_____

_____

_____

Forgiving and Praying in Secret

6. Continue reading in Matthew 6, and reflect on verses 5–14. Where and how are we to pray?

_____

_____

_____

Though there is much to say about prayer, the starting point for all prayer really is forgiveness. And forgiveness is often done so that no one else sees; no one really knows the heartfelt cost.

One of the greatest hindrances that keeps us from doing good things for other people is that people hurt and disappoint us. Stop and think about it for a minute. Have you ever had an idea to do a "random act of kindness" for someone, but then you remembered something she had done or said that hurt you? Perhaps your next thought was, *Why should I do that for her?* I know I have struggled with this. At other times I have felt as if I am always the one giving, and I wonder why someone else can't give to me? These are sorry thoughts but a very real struggle at times. This is why walking in forgiveness toward others ties in so significantly to living a life rich in good works.

I have had times when someone hurt me so badly, and I had to forgive her in my heart over and over and over again. If I hadn't, I would have felt crushed by how hurt I was. In fact, recently a friend (and isn't it always a friend that can hurt you this deeply?) said the most hurtful things to someone else about me, and it came full circle back to my ears. Though her words were somewhat exaggerated, she truly had been pained by things I had and had not done for her. It was perhaps the most painful thing I had ever gone through with a friend. Though we talked it through, I had to discipline my mind not to dwell on and rehearse the pain and betrayal I felt. It seemed as if she were thinking the worst of me instead of somehow believing the best. I knew that if I didn't release this situation, I would be destroyed by it.

This beautiful poem written by my wonderful friend Lorraine Pintus came to mind:

Dear Jesus, my heart is breaking;
I cry out, my Lord, to you.
I know you feel my aching,
For you have been here, too.

You've enjoyed the kisses of a friend;
You've known the wounds as well.
The first brought joy that knew no end,
The other, a living hell.

Jesus, how did you stand it?
The pain is a searing knife.
And yet as the Father planned it,
For them, you gave up your life.

Jesus, I cannot do this . . .
Lead me through this wretched pain.
I give my horror, my hurt to you;
Use it somehow for your gain.

---

7. Have you ever experienced pain and disappointment like I described above? What did that feel like for you?

_____

_____

_____

8. Do you still struggle with letting it go and releasing the frustration, disillusionment, and anger? If so, what do you do when those feelings come up again?

_____

_____

_____

The good thing is that eventually, by persistently forgiving in my heart, my heart is clean toward that person. I can look her in the eye and trust that God is my ultimate Defender and Help. He will vindicate the situation. He will cause life to come forth even in a painful, barren land. He can make all things beautiful if we obey and trust Him to do it. Unforgiveness comes to lodge in our hearts and keeps us from living the lifegiving lifestyle unless we diligently uproot it. Today is a new day, a day when you can live in forgiveness as you have never done before.

9. Read Luke 23:34 and notice how Jesus responded to those who beat and killed Him. What could Jesus have said about these offenders? What did He say instead?

_____

_____

_____

10. Jesus gave a reason for His forgiveness. Write out the phrase He used.

_____

_____

_____

11. Ephesians 4:32 says, "Be kind and compassionate to one another, forgiving each other, just as in Christ God forgave you." What does this verse tell us about *why* we should forgive others?

_____

_____

_____

Acts of Kindness

12. Read Luke 6:27–36. These verses talk about who we show love to, why, and what comes of it. Is it a credit to us to love those who love us? Why or why not?

_____

_____

_____

13. Do you tend to only love those who love you?

_____

_____

_____

[Jesus said,] "Love your enemies! Do good to them! Lend to them! And don't be concerned that they might not repay. Then your reward from heaven will be very great, and you will truly be acting as children of the Most High, for he is kind to the unthankful and to those who are wicked."

LUKE 6:35 (NLT)

14. According to Luke 6:35, how do we show ourselves uniquely to be the "children of the Most High"?

_____

_____

_____

15. When we give to others, what should we expect in return? (Ouch, this hurts!) But if we obey, then what will our reward be like? (Remember, the Bible is full of if/then statements—*if* we obey, *then* we receive the promise, protection, and reward from God Himself.)

_____

_____

_____

16. To whom does God show kindness, according to this verse?

_____

17. Take a few minutes to reflect on God's kindness to you. Write down a few ways you have experienced the kindness of God in your life:

_____

_____

_____

Good Ground

Let's look back now on the passages we've studied this week and examine the lessons we can draw from them.

18. As you studied Matthew 6:1–6, what came to mind about your motives for doing good things for others?

_____

_____

_____

19. Take a few minutes to write out a prayer, asking God to help you do your good works *for His eyes only* and to free you from the trap of needing others' approval and praise.

_____

_____

_____

20. Have you ever had an experience where God rewarded you openly for something you did in secret? Describe the experience.

_____

_____

_____

21. In Luke 23:34 we read Jesus' statement "Father, forgive them, for they do not know what they are doing." How can you apply this statement—"for they do not know what they are doing"— to those who have hurt you?

_____

_____

_____

22. Are you wondering, *How could this person not have known what she was doing to me? Isn't it obvious that what she did/said was so awful?* Ask yourself: What is it that keeps people from realizing how much they've hurt us? (Think about this for a little while. It could change your life!)

_____

_____

_____

23. Friend, take time right now to list people God has called you to release and forgive. This is so important. Stay here in this place until God brings these people to mind. Ask God to reveal this to you. Write out their names below; then write a prayer of forgiveness next to each name.

_____

_____

_____

_____

_____

_____

Forgiveness does not make what the other person did to you okay; it makes *you* okay. You are releasing the right of punishing the other person for the hurt done against you. Keep forgiving that person throughout your day—while you do your laundry, sit through a meeting, drive to an appointment, make the beds, walk the grocery aisles. Walk in that forgiveness toward your offender. True forgiveness is often a process. Don't be discouraged when you feel the pain for the wound; rather, release it again and ask God for His help.

Though this might feel very hard, ask God to bring this person into the path of your daily life so that forgiveness can be given and received. I have done this, and it is amazing how God brought the person into my path. I have physically bumped into a person I needed to forgive whom I hadn't contacted in years, and a supernatural encounter made the connection happen. Anticipate that God will move in this way, and watch and see what happens.

Sometimes this might be impossible, though—for example, if the person has died. (And did you know that people who are no longer here on earth can still have such a hold on us?) You can still forgive in that secret place. You see, the issue is never how that person, dead or alive, *responds to you;* the issue is our obedience in giving and extending forgiveness. God wants us to live freely and beautifully in all our relationships. If we choose to obey, then we will live with liberty. We can forgive others, even those we will never see again this side of eternity, and be freed from their hold on us. Now *that* is true life to our souls!

Fasting in Secret

Did you know that fasting is a very big idea to God? Read Jesus' instructions on fasting in Matthew 6:16–18. A physical fast means going without food for a number of days. This basic exercise in self-denial brings a renewed awareness of your desires and refocuses your attention on God and not your own needs and desires. Yet fasting can also mean more than just going without food for a few days. Heartfelt fasting is often giving up our hopes, dreams, and desires to a God who can be trusted. It is releasing the *control* of how things should happen in our lives and what they should look like. Like a physical fast, a heartfelt fast means denying yourself something that you want so that you can grapple with areas of desire and discipline in your life. This heartfelt fast can look different from one person's life to the next.

For me fasting looked like having four kids, five years old and younger, and dying to myself daily.

For me fasting looked like leaving a job I loved to stay at home full-time with my kids.

For me fasting looked like living where God called us, making several moves, living away from my family, submitting to His timing and ways.

For me fasting looked like being alone when my husband traveled . . . a lot!

For me fasting was and is a daily thing.

24. What about you? What does the fast of your life look like? Perhaps you are fasting the desire for a godly husband, children you long to hold, a career that really pays the bills and brings fulfillment, or a health issue that causes you pain and discomfort daily. List everything that comes to mind.

_____

_____

_____

Now get ready for this . . . Did you know that when you offer all these things to God, it is a beautiful act in His sight, and He will *reward* you for your obedience in persevering? Did you know that heartfelt, godly fasting gets God's attention? Did you know that He is passionate about what we give to Him; that it is precious to Him?

Why? Because you're whispering to God, in secret, that you trust *Him* to meet your needs, to fulfill your heart's longings, to be loving and faithful to you. You are proclaiming that He alone is your rock, your comfort, your avenger. Yes, He is your abundant supply.

And here is the really good news. He will one day reward everything you have placed in His care. It is safe with Him. Actually it has been placed in your eternal bank account. Paul said it perfectly in 2 Timothy 1:12, "That is why I am suffering as I am. Yet I am not ashamed, because I know whom I have believed, and am convinced that he is able *to guard what I have entrusted to him for that day*" (emphasis mine). This concept has so changed my perspective that I almost look forward to my fasting (well, most of the time), because I know that God is giving me more opportunities to grow that future account large and prosperous. My reward may not be seen here on earth, but it will most certainly be given in heaven. He said it; count on it. Don't you just love that!

GOOD FRUIT

25. Write out any ideas for good deeds that have come to your mind during this study. Have you thought of any secret service that God may want you to perform for others but only to be seen by Him? Keep in mind Psalm 62:12, "Surely you will reward each person according to what he has done," and Ephesians 6:7–8, "Serve wholeheartedly, as if you were serving the Lord, not men, because you know that the Lord will reward everyone for whatever good he does." How can you begin the journey of the secret life?

_____

_____

_____

_____

_____

_____

26. List three good things you plan to do for ungrateful and unkind people you know. Remember, it is for His eyes only!

❖

❖

❖

Now, friend, go and do them! Remember, press on; never pull back!

Let us not become weary in doing good, for at the proper time we will reap a harvest if we do not give up. Therefore, as we have opportunity, let us do good to all people, especially to those who belong to the family of believers.

GALATIANS 6:9–10

JOURNAL NOTES

JOURNAL NOTES

JOURNAL NOTES

Nurturing Souls with Beauty and Grace

The Lifegiving Home

"Home . . . where life makes up its mind." Chuck Swindoll

What actually makes a lifegiving home? All of us have moments—or even seasons—when we feel our home atmosphere is anything *but* lifegiving! I have had people come into my home and comment on the peace and order and life they sense there. And I stand there thinking, *Amazing! I was just yelling at the kids to throw the dirty underwear that was under the coffee table into the laundry room and to grab the escaped birds (that the dog was chasing) and put them back in their cage!*

Alas, this is a testament to the supernatural quality of lifegiving. Look at that word: *supernatural*. Above and beyond what is naturally possible. Friend, this is the key—realizing that the beauty and glory of a lifegiving home may express itself outwardly in paint color, fabric design, or a meal of comfort food, but the inner reality is in the *Zoë* life of God!

We have all been in beautiful homes that have no real life. They look fabulous on the exterior (and sometimes the interior, too), but as you dig a little deeper you find there is no real life or loveliness inside. As lifegiving women, we want our outward perception to mirror our inward reality. So how do we start? We start with understanding the *Zoë* life of God and the enemy's intent to keep us from embracing it.

GOOD SEED
Abundant Life in Christ Alone

Lifegiving women are compelled to raise life above mere existence. We know that in order to nurture, love, and care for others, we must thrive, not just survive!

LIFEGIVING, P. 84

1. In John 10:10 Jesus gives us a picture of the kind of life He came to give us. He also warns us about our enemy, the thief. The thief comes to kill, steal, and destroy. Who is the thief Jesus is talking about?

_____

2. Think about people in the world around you. How does the thief kill? How do you see him destroying lives?

_____

_____

_____

3. What does he try to steal from people? (Consider matters of the heart and soul in your answer.)

_____

_____

_____

In John 10:10 Jesus goes on to say that He came to give life abundantly (NASB). This word for life in the Greek is *Zoë*, and it means not only "life" but also "lifegiving." *Zoë* refers to "life as a principle, life in the absolute sense, life as God has it, that which the Father has in Himself, and which He gave to the Incarnate Son to have in Himself, and which the Son manifested in the world."[1]

4. What does Colossians 3:3–4 tell us about Christ, the believer, and life?

_____

5. This is eternal life, and this life is eternal. Do we have this life now, or do we begin it when we die and go to heaven? Read and then paraphrase the following verses in your own words: John 3:15, 5:24; 2 Timothy 1:10; 1 John 3:14.

_____

_____

_____

_____

This life is not merely a principle of power and mobility, however, for it has moral associations which are inseparable from it, as of holiness and righteousness.[2]

6. Based on those same verses, describe the characteristics of this *Zoë* of God. (It's much more than just life here on earth!)

_____

_____

_____

In John 10:10 Jesus explains how He gives this life. He gives it *abundantly!* The Greek word for abundantly is *perissos*. It means to superabound (in quantity or quality), be in excess or superfluous; to be the better, enough and to spare, exceed, excel, increase, be left, redound, remain, over and above.[3] This is the kind of life Jesus said He came to give.

The abundant life Christ gives will look different for each of us. For a single woman, the abundant life of Christ may mean good female friends who are God's promise-keepers to her in moments of loneliness—God's abundance to her in a practical time of need. To a married woman, a household of happy children and a loving marriage partnership—God's abundance in meeting her heart's desires. And to an older woman, rich friendships, meaningful memories, and health—God's abundance to her in a life well lived.

7. For me, the abundant life of Christ looks like joy, contentment, satisfaction, and intentional purpose in my day-to-day living. What does it look like for you?

_____

_____

_____

8. Think deeply about this. List some specific ways Jesus gives this kind of life to us.

_____

_____

_____

God Himself has lifted up beauty as a testimony to His nature by creating a beautiful world.

LIFEGIVING, P. 85

The Beauty of God

As we studied in week 1, lifegiving began in a beautiful garden, and it is natural for women to bring God's life into their homes by expressing beauty. I might like brick red and tan paint on my walls, and you may choose Caribbean blues and sunny yellows. Our different tastes do not matter. These are all beautiful things. Where does all beauty have its origin? (Hint: the One who created every good thing.)

9. Where is the physical expression of God's beauty seen?

_____

_____

_____

10. Read Psalm 19 and Romans 1:18–21. Write out phrases from these passages that describe how creation reveals the beauty of God.

_____

_____

_____

I love living in Colorado. The beauty here is breathtaking. When I'm feeling overwhelmed, stressed, and maxed out on life, I take a walk and breathe in the fresh air and beauty of my surroundings, which testify to the creative power of the Most High God. I love how He makes sunsets, huge pine trees, and burnt red (yes, red!) dirt. Though not all of us get to look at Pikes Peak on a day-to-day basis, we can all see characteristics of God in creation.

11. Imagine being in a remote place, a place where life seems to slow down and the natural beauty is breathtaking (or better yet, go there now if the place is nearby). Look around you. Be still enough to reflect. What does this place communicate to you about God (e.g., His majesty)?

_____

_____

_____

12. Have you ever experienced a moment when all of creation seemed to shout the beauty of God? How did that moment affect you? Did it inspire you to worship Him?

_____

_____

_____

Psalm 96:6 says, "Splendor and majesty are before Him, strength and beauty are in His sanctuary" (NASB). The Hebrew word for *beauty* here is *tiph'arah* or *tiph'ereth*, and it means "beauty—finery, used of garments, jewels; glory, used of rank; renown, as an attribute of God; honor, of the nation of Israel; glorying, boasting, used of an individual."[4]

13. God's beauty is perfect. It is rich, full, glorious, and even ornamental! I cannot wait to see it for myself. With what eyes do we "see" God now? Read Ephesians 1:17–23 to find out.

_____

_____

_____

Bob Sorge wrote in *The Fire of God's Love:*

> Let me suggest for your meditation that God's most intrinsic quality is that He is beautiful. Every other quality emanates from His beauty, which means that every other quality of His nature is also beautiful. A thing is beautiful only if God says so. If it's beautiful to God, it's beautiful. Sin has distorted our ability to perceive beauty. The regenerate man is awakened to appreciate the beauty of God.[5]

As we grow in love and lifegiving, which is beautiful to the Lord, we become more and more attractive in His sight, for we are taking on the very nature of Christ. Then we can agree with Moses when he cried, "And let the beauty of the Lord our God be upon us" (Psalm 90:17, KJV).

He is our source. He is the quintessence of all breathtaking beauty and abundant life. Praise God!

The Well That Never Runs Dry

Doesn't all this lifegiving in the home—beautifying, decorating, preparing, not to mention cleaning up—leave us feeling spent and empty sometimes? These are the times when we don't just need a drink of living water; we need to tap into the wellspring. Jesus once talked to a woman who had lived a hard life, and He claimed to be the living water, a well that will never run dry.

14. Read John 4:4–15. Now pretend that you are the woman at the well. In your own words, write out a conversation (based on Jesus' conversation with the woman in John 4) that *you* might have with Jesus. If you were this woman, what might you want to say to Him?

_____

_____

_____

If you have time, read the following accounts of what happened to other women at springs or wells—Hagar in Genesis 16:6–14, 21:14–21; Rebekah in Genesis 24:13–26; and Rachel in Genesis 29:1–12. Keep in mind that collecting water at the well was an integral part of daily life and a routine chore for these women. Notice how each of these women encountered God at the well. Be encouraged that you can encounter God in the midst of mundane housework.

Good Ground

Let's look back now on the passages we've studied this week and prayerfully consider the impact of God's Word—the good seed—in our hearts.

15. Think back to John 10:10. How has Satan tried to steal, kill, and destroy in your life? Often it comes through sin we have committed and sin that has been committed against us. Though it can be very difficult to realize, it's in this place that Christ wants to meet us. And it is also in this place that we see His unending faithfulness. Journal your story below.

_____

_____

_____

_____

16. Describe the time when you first put your faith in Christ and how you experienced the *Zoë*— life—of God.

_____

_____

_____

17. Write out a list of ways that you have experienced the abundant life of Christ. If you are having a difficult time with this, make your list a prayer list of how you wish to experience His abundance. Refer back to the description of what the word *abundantly* means in John 10:10.

_____

_____

_____

18. When have you felt your own spiritual well was running dry? Why do you think that happened?

_____

_____

_____

19. How do you connect with Christ as the continual source of lifegiving water? What can you do to grow in that type of fellowship with Him?

_____

_____

_____

GOOD FRUIT

20. Creation is a physical expression of many of God's attributes and qualities. Describe how your home is a physical expression of your attributes or qualities.

_____

_____

_____

21. Just as our homes show our characteristics, so God's home says something about Him, too. Wait until you see what God has planned for us! Read John 14:1–3. Describe the kind of heavenly home you think God is preparing for us. (See Revelation 21:1–4 for more insight.)

_____

_____

_____

No matter what we do out in the world, no matter what our lifestyle, almost all of us have a place we call home. Creating a lifegiving atmosphere in our home nurtures the souls of [all who come there].

LIFEGIVING, P. 86

What qualities do you wish your home had? A few of the home-life characteristics I continue to work on are infusing my home with laughter, life, and acceptance (okay, and a bit more order too!). Now, friend, there are many times this grumpy mom doesn't even come close to hitting that bull's-eye mark. But we must have a mark to shoot for, or we will never hit anything!

So set your "mark," and think about what your dream home atmosphere looks like. Really go for it! Dream big, and lay out your heart's desires. After you write out your list, go back and pray through it, asking God to make it a reality in your life. Pray about each item. Ask God to make it a reality in your home.

My sister Twyla has been a third-grade teacher for almost twenty-five years. Twyla says that successful, life-changing teaching embraces one main component: the lifelong takeaway. What does she mean by that? Twyla feels strongly that "many years later, children might not remember what

I taught them, what curriculum I used, or the pristine order of the classroom modular. But they will always remember the way I made them feel." I just love that! Yes, and those we care about will remember the very same thing about our homes.

22. List five ways you want your family and friends to feel when they are in your home. Remember, we are not talking about perfected images here. We are dreaming of a life well lived, in the everyday-ness of our homes.

❖

❖

❖

❖

❖

23. List three new ways you plan to bring beauty, glory, and ornament to your home this year. Now start simply, but simply start!

❖

❖

❖

JOURNAL NOTES

JOURNAL NOTES

JOURNAL NOTES

Gathered and Tied with Heartstrings

LIFEGIVING IN FRIENDSHIPS

Would you like to read the story of a beautiful relationship between female friends? Turn to Luke 1:35–58 and enter into the first-century world of the Middle East, where two cousins are about to experience the height of joy in their relationship. This is the story of Mary and Elizabeth.

This passage expresses not only Mary's song—also known as the Magnificat—but an unwritten song as well. Can you hear the soft sound of a beautiful melody of friendship? As we read about the interaction between Mary and Elizabeth, the words are like the lyrics of a heart-to-heart ballad of friendship between women.

If we listen carefully, we can discern the background theme of their interaction. Do you hear it? It is the *glory of God* expressed in the lives of two physical as well as spiritual lifegivers. Mary runs to Elizabeth to rejoice over what God is doing in *her*, even as Elizabeth responds to Mary and exults in what God is doing in *her*. Between the lines, they exhibit the qualities of one of the most incredible relationships between two women in Scripture. Here we have a picture of what God intends for women as they share their lives with each other.

As you begin to unpack this passage, bask in the glory of this relationship. Ask yourself, "How can I be that kind of friend?"

GOOD SEED

1. Read Luke 1:35–58. Write out what the angel told Mary about her cousin Elizabeth (see Luke 1:36).

_____

_____

_____

2. Where did Mary go right after the angel left her?

_____

_____

3. In your own words, summarize what Elizabeth said to Mary when she heard her greeting.

_____

_____

_____

4. How did Elizabeth's unborn baby respond?

_____

_____

5. In your own words, summarize Mary's response to Elizabeth's affirmation of what God had done for her (Luke 1:46–55).

_____

_____

_____

Proverbs 17:17 says, "A friend is always loyal, and a brother is born to help in time of need" (NLT). In the *New American Standard* (NASB) this verse reads, "A friend loves at all times, and a brother is born for adversity."

6. What does it mean that a friend loves at all times?

_____

_____

More often than not, we experience—and we ourselves show—unfaithfulness in friendship. Proverbs 20:6 says, "Many a man claims to have unfailing love, but a faithful man who can find?"

7. Explain what you think this proverb is saying about relationships.

_____

_____

Proverbs 27:6 says, "Wounds from a friend are better than many kisses from an enemy" (NLT). Some define an enemy as anyone who does not have your interests at heart. Wow! I have always had a much more sinister view of what an enemy might be like. This definition includes a lot more people than I'd originally thought. When Jesus told us to love our enemies (Matthew 5:44), He meant loving those who essentially do not care much about us.

8. Describe the wounds of a friend.

_____

_____

_____

9. Describe the kisses of an enemy. In what ways are these different from and/or similar to the wounds of a friend?

_____

_____

_____

GOOD GROUND

Let's look back now on the passages we've studied this week and examine the lessons we can draw from them.

10. Theologians suggest that Mary was a very young woman—possibly only an adolescent. We know that she was still single (though pledged to be married to Joseph). How do you think Mary felt when she heard Elizabeth's affirmation of her unforeseen pregnancy?

_____

_____

_____

11. Does that touch something in your heart? Describe a time when someone affirmed something that God was doing in your life that others didn't seem to understand.

_____

_____

_____

12. Have you ever had an "Elizabeth" in your life? How about a "Mary"? Describe her.

_____

_____

_____

13. How have you experienced the love of a friend who was faithful and loyal to you? What did that do for you in difficult times?

_____

_____

_____

14. If you have never had that kind of friend, write out a prayer asking God to give you a faithful friend.

_____

_____

_____

15. Describe a time when you have experienced the wound of a friend. How did you respond?

_____

_____

_____

16. In Luke 22:21–22, Jesus is at the Last Supper with His twelve disciples, and He announces to His closest friends that one of them will betray Him. He says, "But here at this table, sitting among us as a friend, is the man who will betray me" (NLT). Have you ever been betrayed by a close friend? Describe your experience.

_____

_____

_____

If you have never prayed through that experience, take time right now to pray for the Lord to touch your heart and to help you forgive that person. Keep in mind that Judas wasn't just one of the crowd; he was one of the inner twelve! Jesus knows exactly how you feel.

The Seasons of Friendship

In my book *Lifegiving,* I described that most friendships seem to go through three basic phases. First is the honeymoon season, where all we see is what we like in a person, and we don't really notice too many faults. Then we enter the disappointment season, when we start to rub each other the wrong way, and the other's weaknesses seem to come under the magnifying glass. Honestly, this is where most friendships die and are buried. But those who press through it come out into the light of true lifegiving friendship. In order to get there, we must realize that true fellowship is based on walking in the light together.

17. First John 1:5–10 gives us some key insights on how our true connection, or fellowship with one another, is based on "walking in the light" together. What does it mean to walk in the darkness? What does it mean to walk in the light?

_____

_____

_____

18. How do walking in darkness and walking in light relate to each other? to God?

_____

_____

_____

19. Why does true fellowship require friends to walk in the light together?

_____

_____

_____

20. There is an old saying that goes, "To have a friend, be a friend." How can you begin to *be* the kind of friend you want to *have*?

_____

_____

_____

If you are like me, you may have had times in your life when you have clung to friends and looked primarily to them to meet your emotional needs. Can friends meet the deep needs of our hearts? Yes, they can. But I have discovered that there is a big difference between allowing *God* to orchestrate how my heart needs will be met through others and *my* personally choreographing that. Wow! What a difference there is between those two. Our friends, dear and wonderful as they may be, can essentially become idols when we look to them first instead of looking to God.

21. Have you ever picked up the phone to call a friend when you should have dropped to your knees to call on God? (I sure have!) Describe your experience.

_____

_____

_____

Now take some time to surrender that to God. Ask your heavenly Father, the Lover of your soul, the only completely true and faithful One, to become first in your life, your all in all. Truly He is the only Jehovah-Jirah, our Provider. Only He can orchestrate the meeting of your deepest heart needs. Take a few moments to pray and pour your heart out to God. "Trust in him at all times, O people; pour out your hearts to him, for God is our refuge" (Psalm 62:8).

GOOD FRUIT

22. Describe a time when you experienced a godly connection—as Mary and Elizabeth did—with a friend because of a shared experience in the Lord.

_____

_____

_____

Mary and Elizabeth rejoiced with one another over what God was doing in each of them. Did you notice how Elizabeth—though she was the older woman in the story—humbled herself and acknowledged the honor that was due to her younger cousin? God had given Mary the great honor of being the mother of _her_ Savior.

23. How have you rejoiced, or how can you plan to rejoice, with someone to whom God is giving a more exciting ministry or a bigger responsibility than He's given you? (Ouch, this one really gets to the heart of our competitive sin nature.)

_____

_____

_____

24. Have you ever felt your heart well up with praise to the Lord for something He was doing or had done in your life? This is what Mary was doing when she vocalized her song, called the Magnificat (Luke 1:46–55). Write out your own "Magnificat." What would be the words of your song of praise to the Lord?

_____

_____

_____

Forgiveness and Healing

Another beautiful aspect of lifegiving friendships is extending healing to one another. James 5:15–17 says, "And the prayer offered in faith will make the sick person well; the Lord will raise him up. If he has sinned, he will be forgiven. Therefore confess your sins to each other and pray for each other so that you may be healed. The prayer of a righteous man is powerful and effective." Did you catch that? Verse 15 tells us that if we confess our sins to the Lord, we will be forgiven. Verse 16 extends that by adding that when we confess our sins to one another, we will be *healed*!

There is a difference between knowing you are forgiven and experiencing the beauty and wholeness of being healed. That's where the body of Christ comes in. Yes, that is where *we* come in! When we put ourselves in humble positions of sharing our brokenness and also accepting the brokenness of others—without judgment and shame—we are actually acting like Christ Himself. As we embrace each other this way, we release control over how we think God should deal with someone else and how the outcome of her situation should look. We are able to live in freedom and peace.

You see, dear friend, when we really love the body of Christ, we must embrace and extend mercy to the one who is wounded, leading her to the open arms of the Great Physician. Yes, all of us have been called to the ministry of confession and restoration. This is honoring to our Lord, the eternal Healer.

Let me also address another issue that you might be struggling with right now. Perhaps you have confessed your sin to a friend, and, instead of open arms and forgiveness, you were greeted with rejection and shame. Sadly, this does happen. I know, for it has happened to me, and it was one of the most painful experiences I have ever gone through in a friendship.

If this is what you have experienced, though it is painful and very difficult, release your friend and pray for her. Why? Because I have learned that friends who respond to you in this manner are actually deeply wounded themselves, and often they are simply unable to grant you this type of unconditional love. Sometimes they may choose not to, but often they actually can't. Why? Because they have never truly experienced the mercy and grace of God. They are imprisoned by their judgments and unforgiveness and do not even realize it.

So if you find yourself in this position, what should you do?

Forgive her.

Pray for God's blessing on her.

And then . . . you let it go. Release her, the words, the misunderstanding, and the pain, and know that God is working all things together for your good (Romans 8:28). Trust me, it really works.

25. Think back now to your lifegiving friends (and aren't they worth their weight in gold?). What was the fruit in your life as a result of your confession to them? Did you experience freedom in a real way?

_____

_____

_____

26. How have you been a lifegiving friend to others?

_____

_____

_____

27. List three people who have been lifegiving friends to you. Write out a sentence that expresses what makes you feel that way about each of them. Now take time today to call her or write her a note to let her know how amazing she is!

_____

_____

_____

28. In the end, we have One who is the most faithful Friend of all, the Lord Jesus Christ. Proverbs 18:24 says, "There are 'friends' who destroy each other, but a real friend sticks closer than a brother" (NLT). This is the kind of unfailing Friend that Christ is. Write out a prayer of dedication to the Lord, your ultimate, lifegiving Friend.

_____

_____

_____

_____

_____

JOURNAL NOTES

JOURNAL NOTES

JOURNAL NOTES

A Message We Give Others About Their Value

LIFEGIVING THROUGH HOSPITALITY

"Americans are just beginning to regard food the way the French always have. Dinner is not what you do in the evening before something else. Dinner is the evening."

ART BUCHWALD, AMERICAN JOURNALIST

"Ponder well on this point: The pleasant hours of our life are all connected by a more or less tangible line, with some memory of the table."

CHARLES PIERRE MONSELET, NINETEENTH-CENTURY FRENCH AUTHOR

"The discovery of a new dish does more for human happiness than the discovery of a new star."

ANTHELME BRILLAT-SAVARIN, EIGHTEENTH-CENTURY FRENCH AUTHOR

Well, friends, let's get down to brass tacks about the reality of opening our homes—and giving from our hearts—to others in hospitality. (Keep in mind, opening any part of ourselves to others is a place of vulnerability.) Over the last twenty years, I probably have invited hundreds of guests into my home. Sometimes the take-away was downright wonderful. Other times the experience left me feeling like less than a modern-day Martha!

Opening our homes and giving to others has its highs and lows. The highs are the joys of preparation and decoration; seeing the pleasure in people's faces as they find the candles lit and fresh flowers on the table; your guests' delight as they bite into a simple though luscious meal prepared just for them; the sound of laughter and good conversation; the sharing of life that reverberates in your soul even after they've gone. These are some of the highs of hospitality in the home.

Ah, but let's be *real*. These highs have a counterpart. The lows of entertaining and opening your home and preparing a place for others are also genuine. There is the mental and physical effort that goes into preparation and cleanup. (Now I must tell you that my husband, Butch, said to me years ago, "Tammy, if you cook it, I will clean it!" That's a good deal, isn't it? As far as I am concerned, making the mess is the fun part!) Then you have to take into account the weariness you may feel after everyone is gone and the possibility that your guests may not seem to notice what you have gone through for them. And then there is the granddaddy of all the lows, like nails on the chalkboard of our fleshly nature. Our hearts cry out for reciprocation; we want others to do for us what we have done for them! The fact of the matter is that very few people will invite us over in return. It may be as low as one out of twenty who will invite us over for dinner after we have had them. After all our work, this can feel very disappointing.

Does it sound like we are whining? Have you ever heard that old playground song "Nobody loves me, everybody hates me, I'm going to eat some worms!" (Some of you may be too young to remember that!) I must confess, sometimes that is how I felt in years past, after everyone had gone home and I was standing at the sink at 11:00 P.M. doing the dishes. (That was before Butch and I struck the "I make it, you clean it up" treaty.)

The etiquette books may say, "When someone has you over, you should reciprocate." Yet we have to recognize the difference between godly hospitality and worldly entertaining. The hard truth of hospitality is that few will return the invitation. So how do we keep inviting people in without the affirmation and encouragement of being invited back? How do we keep giving when we don't feel appreciated? Does it really matter?

Over the years I have found a new answer to this dilemma. When we develop God's perspective and God's heart for hospitality, we can change the world in which we find ourselves.

Anyone can entertain with a few tips from Mom or Grandma, the average etiquette book, and a halfway decent cookbook, or by watching *Emeril Live*. (He is one messy, wild, crazy cook! And the way he just loves his own cooking—we are all about that.) Lifegiving hospitality may involve good books and role models, but it starts with one Book—God's Word—and a work of the Spirit in our hearts. The greater reality of hospitality is that we are not having people over to be invited back. We are having them over to give them a message about their value. In worldly entertaining, it is easy to trumpet our own sense of worth. In godly hospitality, it is always about our guests—how they can be loved, ministered to, encouraged, enriched, and refreshed while they are in our homes.

In a way, this is like the invitation Jesus referred to in His parable about the kingdom of heaven, in which the people who were originally invited to dinner did not even show up. (At least we hope our guests are willing to come!) Let's see the response of the host in this parable and uncover a few principles for godly hospitality.

Good Seed

Read Matthew 22:1–14 and Luke 14:15–24, and answer the following questions about these similar parables.

1. Who did the servants first call to the wedding banquet?

_____

_____

_____

2. Notice that the invited guests were *unwilling* to come. What were these guests doing that kept them from coming to the feast? List the activities.

_____

_____

_____

3. How did the king react to the outright refusal of his generous invitation?

_____

_____

_____

4. Where did he send his servants to invite new guests? Describe the new guests.

_____

_____

_____

In the verses preceding the second parable, Luke 14:12–14, Jesus issues a great challenge, striking at the heart of kingdom hospitality. Here Jesus speaks to our fleshly desire that our guests reciprocate our kindness.

5. Read Luke 14:12–14. What does Jesus expose here about the desire to have our guests reciprocate?

_____

_____

_____

6. What kind of guests does He recommend we invite instead?

_____

_____

_____

7. Where does true repayment for our hospitality come from?

_____

_____

_____

That passage challenges the oven mitts off my natural approach to hospitality! God's Word has even more to say on the subject, so let's keep reading.

8. In Romans 12:13 and Hebrews 13:1–3, with whom are we instructed to share?

_____

_____

_____

9. "Share with God's people who are in need. Practice hospitality" (Romans 12:13). The end of this verse says something critical about hospitality. I believe this statement dispels the erroneous notion that hospitality is just a gift that only a few people have. What does this verse tell *all of us* to do when it comes to hospitality? Rewrite the instructions in CAPITAL LETTERS below.

_____

Dinner with Jesus

In the Gospels we find some specific instructions about how we should approach serving others in and through hospitality. Read about the two famous sisters Mary and Martha in the passage below. Let's discover what Jesus wanted them to learn.

As Jesus and his disciples were on their way, he came to a village where a woman named Martha opened her home to him. She had a sister called Mary, who sat at the Lord's feet listening to what he said. But Martha was distracted by all the preparations that had to be made. She came to him and asked, "Lord, don't you care that my sister has left me to do the work by myself? Tell her to help me!"

"Martha, Martha," the Lord answered, "you are worried and upset about many things, but only one thing is needed. Mary has chosen what is better, and it will not be taken away from her."

LUKE 10:38–42

10. When Jesus entered the village, what did Martha do?

_____

_____

_____

11. Once Jesus was in their home, how did Mary respond to Him?

_____

_____

_____

12. Think of all the preparations that go into a meal, especially in ancient times, and write out the activities that you imagine Martha may have been doing. How consumed by her preparations was she?

_____

_____

_____

13. In your own words, relay Martha's complaint to Jesus.

_____

_____

14. Write out Jesus' exact reply to her.

_____

_____

15. What made Martha's approach to serving necessary?

_____

_____

GOOD GROUND

Let's look back now on the passages we've studied this week and examine the lessons we can draw from them.

16. What is the difference between godly hospitality and worldly entertaining?

_____

_____

_____

17. How can this understanding affect your approach to having people in your home?

_____

_____

_____

18. Do you practice hospitality on a regular basis? Whom do you usually invite?

_____

_____

_____

19. How regularly do your guests reciprocate the invitation?

_____

_____

_____

20. Describe a time when you were, like Martha, distracted by all your preparations. What did that look like, and feel like, for you?

_____

_____

_____

21. Describe a time when you were, like Mary, able to choose what is "better" and truly sit at the feet of your guests, honor them, and give them your attention. How did that make you feel? (This can be challenging for me, especially when I think I have so many splashy ideas for a fabulous party and lots of *stuff* to get done.)

_____

_____

_____

GOOD FRUIT

22. How do you "practice hospitality"?

_____

_____

_____

What fresh new ideas can you think of to practice hospitality in your home? I've listed a few below to get you started.

If the idea of making a full meal stresses you out, start simple. Try making a salad (begin with a bag of prewashed, fresh-cut lettuce). Add some oranges, grapes, and sun-dried tomatoes. Buy a lasagna or other frozen entrée from the grocery story. (You can even put it in your own pan. After all, it is home-cooked!) And make the Maltby cake for dessert. (See p. 146 in my book *Lifegiving*.)

Invite friends over for coffee and dessert. Here is one of my new favorite (easy!) desserts. Take store-bought brownies and cut them into bite-sized pieces. Spread Cool Whip® and ice cream over the top of the brownie bites and layer it all with several kinds of berries (blackberries, blueberries, and raspberries). Serve it on a large, crystal pedestal holder and top it off with sparklers. (My friend Jenny did this for me for one of my birthdays, and she let me keep the crystal holder as my gift.) This is an easy and fun recipe, and trust me—no one will ever forget it!

Throw an appetizer party! Ask everyone to bring their favorite appetizer and a copy of the recipe for everyone else who will be there. It's so fun to taste everything and to get the mouth-watering recipes to add to your own collection. And the best part is that you need only provide the drinks. Try making sparkling white pear juice. Mix white pear juice with seltzer water (equal parts), frozen white grapes, and a mint leaf. Greet your guests at the door with this snappy drink in a long-stem glass. They'll know immediately that the evening will be wonderfully fun!

Try an easy theme dinner, like homemade pizzas with lots of fun topping ideas. (Kids are crazy about this idea—it's fun and wonderfully messy!) Another option is taco salads. Buy taco shells at the store and have friends bring the toppings (peppers, lettuce, meat, olives, tomatoes, etc.). Feel free to mix it up and have fun with the themes. Buy already-made ingredients when you can and add your own touch of fun and taste! Have fun, and don't be so concerned about perfection. It is *comfort* we are after, and, for most people, fun feels like comfort!

Check for other tips on how to start in *Lifegiving: Discovering the Secrets to a Beautiful Life*.

23. Now share with one another your top two cooking and hospitality tips!

_____

_____

_____

_____

_____

_____

These are just a few fun, creative ideas to get you started. While I enjoy a wonderful sit-down dinner, for many women this feels a bit overwhelming. But these easy, snappy ideas will get you moving in the right direction.

Who should be your guests? Start with people with whom you want to spend time and develop a relationship. I love the fact that Jesus was always inviting Himself to other people's homes. Isn't that a great revelation of God? He knew that by sitting and supping together, life happened! Healing, hope, forgiveness, laughter, and insights were shared. His companions' eternal conditions were changed—all over braised lamb and pita bread!

Bring a little life into your home. Remember, start simply . . . but simply start!

24. As we learned, our guest list sometimes needs to include those who cannot reciprocate—the needy ones—as Jesus mentioned in the parable of the wedding feast. List some ideas and people that come to mind.

_____

_____

_____

Just start with one. Don't get caught up in grandiose plans for a year-long plan of hospitality. Begin with one simple evening. You might be wonderfully surprised at the results. Give this to the Lord in prayer, and, yes, as always, make a plan. And get ready to enjoy! In fact, I would love to hear from you—how your evening went, how lives were changed, and how you enjoyed your beautiful (but messy) lifegiving. Visit my Web site—www.lifegivingtoday.com—and e-mail your story to me at tammymaltby@aol.com.

JOURNAL NOTES

JOURNAL NOTES

JOURNAL NOTES

Stand Up and Be Counted!

A Few Good Lifegivers

Remember the parable about the master who sent his servants to invite guests to the banquet, and no one would come (Matthew 22:1–14; Luke 14:15–24)? Were the guests too busy to eat cake? Who could possibly be too busy to come and eat cake? So the master said, "Go out to the roads and country lanes and make them come in, so that my house will be full" (Luke 14:23).

Why am I bringing this up again? After all, haven't we covered food and parties enough? (Ah, never enough, . . .) There is another powerful truth in Jesus' parable, and it is worth our attention as we finish our study together. It is our take-away, our final point to ponder. Are you ready?

Many are called, but few are chosen.

We have all been called by God in Christ into this relationship of receiving and giving, into this intimate place with the eternal Lifegiver, who alone transforms us into the lifegiving women we were designed to be. We are called. *But only a few of us will heed that call and follow it.* Dear friends, will you stand up with us and be counted among them—the few, the brave, the humble?

Let's look together at the lives of two amazing lifegivers whose stories are told in Scripture. Dig deep and unearth the hidden treasures in their lives. They didn't live flawless lives, and that is why centuries later we can relate to them. They gave life to those around them, despite their brokenness, and we continue to praise them today.

Good Seed
Sarai—"She that strives too much"

Read Genesis 17:1–21. In this passage God is reaffirming His covenant with Abraham. Sarah will bear a child in her old age, and the baby will be named Isaac. God will carry this forth—*literally*—through Sarah's bearing of Isaac. Through Isaac, God's covenant will be established (17:21).

1. Abraham received the promise; Sarah carried it (Isaac) and brought it forth. How was Sarah a lifegiver in this story, physically as well as spiritually?

_____

_____

_____

God has a thing about names. In God's economy, a name has much to say about someone's character. Sarah was the new name God gave to Sarai. *Sarah* means "princess," for God saw her as the one who would bear many kings by first bearing Isaac. Before God named her, she was called *Sarai*, which some scholars believe means "she that strives." In Genesis 16:3–6, Sarai made the biggest mistake of her life. This woman was destined to be one of the most significant and influential lifegivers of all time, but she couldn't wait for God to do what He had said He would do. She thought she would help Him out a little bit. (How many of us have ever tried that?)

2. Read Genesis 16:3–6. Describe Sarai's big mistake.

_____

_____

_____

3. How did that play out? What happened to Hagar and Ishmael (see Genesis 16:7–16; 21:8–21)?

_____

_____

_____

In Genesis 21:8–9 we read the beginning of the ongoing struggle between the son of promise (Isaac) and the son of Sarai's striving (Ishmael).

4. Consider this: The Arabs have descended from Ishmael and the Jews from Isaac. Describe the ongoing consequences even today of Sarai's trying to fulfill God's promise.

_____

_____

_____

5. Did Sarah's interference ultimately stop God's plan?

_____

_____

_____

6. What enduring message about Sarah do we find in 1 Peter 3:1–6? Write out the instructions for us as lifegiving women that you find in this passage.

_____

_____

_____

7. How is Sarah an example to us today, regardless of whether we are married or single?

_____

_____

_____

The Shunammite woman— "A fearful dream confronted"

Read the story of the Shunammite woman in 2 Kings 4:8–37; 8:1–6.

Of all the women in Scripture, the Shunammite woman is perhaps the most inspiring to me personally. She is a woman who lived life well. She was a respected member of her community, married a long time to the man she loved. She invited the great prophet Elisha to stay with them each time he passed by.

You will find four unnamed women in the second book of Kings—the widowed wife of a prophet (4:1–7), the Shunammite woman (4:8–37; 8:1–6), Naaman's wife's slave girl (5:2–3), and the woman of Samaria (6:25–33.) I find this very interesting. All of these women struggled to see how God would deliver them from something they feared in the future. Each was presented with a forbidding life challenge—to believe that God will show up, that He will come through for them, that He can take the most unlikely circumstances and bring forth life. The Shunammite woman discovered how God doles out His faithfulness—if you have the faith to believe, and you're willing to deal with your disappointed heart, He will always prove to be faithful.

Let's consider three insights from the Shunammite woman's life.

1) BE HONEST.

When the prophet Elisha asked what he could do for her to repay her wonderful hospitality, she simply responded, "I have a home among my own people" (2 Kings 4:13), meaning, "I am happy and content and am in need of nothing." Though this sounded spiritually noteworthy, this statement was simply untrue. I know that I have lived this way far too often. Though my heart was breaking, when someone asked me how I was doing, I replied, "Everything is just great!" Being honest about our condition can often make us feel vulnerable and so out of control.

2) UNEARTH THE DREAM.

Elisha discovered through his servant, Gehazi, that the woman indeed had a need, though she would not even acknowledge it. When the prophet told her that she would give birth to a son, she replied, "No, my lord. . . . Don't mislead your servant, O man of God!" (2 Kings 4:16).

I am convinced that she had put to death her heart's dream and was certain she'd never unearth it again. Yes, she longed for a child, but she had been disappointed so many times before that she could no longer even dare to hope. The prophet unearthed not only the sudden reminder of her heart's desire but also her deep fear that she would have to deal with the disappointment of being unfulfilled once again. It was simply more than she could bear.

3) RUN TO GOD.

She gave birth to a son. The prophet's word came true. She cradled the greatest dream of her heart in her arms. But before long, her greatest fear came true, too. The woman feared that if she did receive the desire of her heart and enjoy such deep satisfaction, somehow it would be taken from her. This horrible sorrow did come to pass, and the young boy died.

But the story did not stop there, for she was an amazing woman of courage. She pressed past her greatest fear and ran to the Source of all hope. She set out to find the man of God, and he came. He prayed for the child, and God restored the child to life. Not only that, but Elisha also warned the woman of a coming seven-year famine, and she heeded his warning and left home. When she returned, the king ordered that all of her land be restored to her. God provided for her at every turn.

8. Does this sound painfully close to your heart? What dream have you given up and buried? Are you afraid of being disappointed once again? Does the fear of disappointment outweigh the fear of living without your dream fulfilled?

_____

_____

_____

Perhaps your buried dream looks like a lifelong marriage partner, a child you can carry and hold in your arms, a strong and healthy body, a husband who actually loves and respects you, or a life that simply doesn't carry so much disappointment and rejection.

9. Though it is hard to begin unearthing our dreams, describe your unmet needs and disappointments to God. Oh, this is so hard! Yes, I know. But I believe this is where true intimacy with Jesus starts. Be honest. He longs to hear the desires of your heart.

_____

_____

_____

Now ask God to help you to live well while you are waiting. And remember that you are waiting for something! God knows full well your desires and needs. It is no big deal for God to bring an Elisha into the life of an obedient lifegiving woman. He did it for the notable woman of Shunem. He wants to do it for you! Count on it—but remember that His provision may come in unexpected forms.

Good Ground

For our final Good Ground section, we will do a little different spade-work. Let's use this time to plow up any fallow ground in our hearts that would hinder us from being the lifegiving women we were designed to be.

Take time to address the following questions. This is a place to ponder and reflect on your life as a lifegiver. Ask the Holy Spirit to show you and help you address the needs in your life. With loving abandon, fall into the strong arms of the ultimate Lifegiver. He will take all the broken pieces in your life and create something new in their place. He is so amazing!

10. How are the lessons you have been learning in this study beginning to show in your everyday life?

_____

_____

_____

11. Are there points we have studied that you are resisting, or areas of pride that are making you unteachable? What are those? Again, take time to surrender those in prayer.

_____

_____

_____

12. Do you know of an area of your life where you know what you should do but don't want to do it? What is holding you up? Consider asking a sister in Christ to pray with you for victory in that area (James 5:16).

_____

_____

_____

Let's move now to some tough questions that relate to your relationship with God and with others. These questions are not meant to heave condemnation in your direction. I fail daily in many of these areas. But to be a lifegiving woman that lives freely with passion and beauty, you must look at each of these with painstaking honesty. Brace yourself and walk into the light!

- Am I consciously or unconsciously creating the impression that I am better than I really am?
- Am I honest in all my acts and words, or do I exaggerate?
- Am I spending time in God's Word on a daily (regular) basis, and am I getting something out of it?
- Am I spending regular time in prayer?
- Do I expect God to really answer my heart's desire?
- Is there anyone I have not forgiven or am struggling to forgive? What am I doing about it?
- Am I self-conscious, self-pitying, or self-justifying?
- Do I try to control and manipulate others (what they think, feel, or do) so that my world feels comfortable? How?
- Have I been completely honest with these questions?

GOOD FRUIT

13. How are you growing to be the lifegiving woman you were created to be?

_____

_____

_____

14. Who do you intend to impact with this message? When do you plan to start? (Suggestion: my dear friend, start today!)

_____

_____

_____

Living the lifegiving lifestyle is not for the faint of heart, but it sure does lead us into the abundant life Christ promises for us. I trust that as we have walked together these few weeks, you have been inspired and encouraged to be all God created you to be. Now, by His unmerited grace and mercy, "live a life of love" (Ephesians 5:1–2). And yes, I will see you along the way!

JOURNAL NOTES

JOURNAL NOTES

JOURNAL NOTES

NOTES

Week 1: Touching Hearts, Touching Lives

1. Anne Ortlund, *Disciplines of the Beautiful Woman* (Dallas, Tex.: Word, 1984), 13.
2. M. R. Vincent, *Word Studies in the New Testament*, Electronic Database (Seattle, Wash.: Biblesoft®, 1997).
3. Amy Carmichael, *Rose from Brier* (Ft. Washington, Pa.: Christian Literature Crusade, 1973), 116.
4. Mother Teresa, *Loving Jesus* (Ann Arbor, Mich.: Servant, 1991), 18.

Week 4: The Ultimate Lifegiver Is Tending Your Garden

1. James Strong, *The New Strong's Exhaustive Numbers and Concordance with Expanded Greek-Hebrew Dictionary* (Seattle, Wash.: Biblesoft®, 1994).

Week 6: Nurturing Souls with Beauty and Grace

1. *Vine's Expository Dictionary of Biblical Words,* ed. W. E. Vine (Nashville: Nelson, 1985), 336-7.
2. Ibid.
3. Maurice A. Robinson, *Indexes to All Editions of Brown-Driver-Briggs Hebrew Lexicon and Thayer's Greek Lexicon* (Lafayette, Ind.: Sovereign Grace Publishers, 2001).
4. Ibid.
5. Bob Sorge, *The Fire of God's Love* (Greenwood, Mo.: Oasis House, 1996), 58.

About the Authors

Tammy Maltby is co-host of Total Living Network's *Aspiring Women*. Through her nationally televised segments and her writing and speaking she mentors women in the lifegiving lifestyle. Her life-altering message of hope and freedom springs from the confidence that God Himself uses the dead places of our lives to create beauty. Tammy lives near the Rocky Mountains of Colorado with her husband, Butch, and their four children, two of whom they have adopted internationally.

Tamra Farah is former executive director of crisis pregnancy centers in San Diego, California and Columbus, Ohio and is a freelance writer and homemaker, and has served in the women's ministry at her church in Colorado Springs, Colorado. She and her husband, Barry, lead The Barnabas Center, which provides leadership symposiums for emerging Christian leaders. Tamra has been instrumental in the development and support of local charities, mentor programs, and charter schools. She and Barry have two children.

SINCE 1894, Moody Publishers has been dedicated to equip and motivate people to advance the cause of Christ by publishing evangelical Christian literature and other media for all ages, around the world. Because we are a ministry of the Moody Bible Institute of Chicago, a portion of the proceeds from the sale of this book go to train the next generation of Christian leaders.

If we may serve you in any way in your spiritual journey toward understanding Christ and the Christian life, please contact us at www.moodypublishers.com.

"All Scripture is God-breathed and is useful for teaching, rebuking, correcting and training in righteousness, so that the man of God may be thoroughly equipped for every good work."
—2 TIMOTHY 3:16, 17

MOODY
PUBLISHERS

THE NAME YOU CAN TRUST®

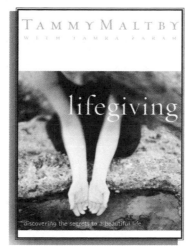

LIFEGIVING JOURNAL TEAM

ACQUIRING EDITOR:
Elsa Mazon

COPY EDITOR & INTERIOR DESIGN:
The Livingstone Corporation

BACK COVER COPY:
Paige Drygas, The Livingstone Corporation

COVER DESIGN:
Journey Group

PRINTING AND BINDING:
Color House Graphics Inc.

The typeface for the text of this book is
ITC Cheltenham